UNCONDITIONAL MONEY

UNCONDITIONAL MONEY

A Magical Journey
Into the Heart of Abundance

By David Cates

Buffalo Press
Willamina, Oregon

DEDICATION

For my Mother and Father,
who gave me everything they had,

and for Jean-Francois,
who believed in the dream before it was visible.

ACKNOWLEDGEMENTS

For their feedback and encouragement during the manuscript process, a special thank you to: Jean-Francois Benoist, Joyce Marvel-Benoist, Strange de Jim, Christopher Grey, Barbara Selvaggi, Jenean Hess, Karen Gehne, Sue Bronson, Nancy and Todd Skowrup, Aaron Garmon, Marcia Jones, my parents Paul and Dolores Cates, my brother Jim, and my sisters Diane, Judy and Eileen. They didn't always know what hit them, but they responded from their hearts.

Two trees are being planted for every tree used in making this book.

PART ONE:

HEAVEN

- $ -

AN INVITATION

Once upon a time, I asked the richest people in this world to teach me about money. My private tutors ranged from business leaders to world-class hookers, Arab moguls to Japanese billionaires, movie stars to U.S. presidents. While frangipani blossoms soaked the ocean air with sweet perfume, we talked of life and love in an enchanted villa by the sea.

In the spirit of aloha, I asked each of my teachers to share with me a secret about money. Their answers shattered every preconception I had ever had about the sources of abundance and success. As their voices rose above the bubbling jacuzzi, I leaned against an ancient palm and scribbled notes. At that time, I was a private butler in paradise, on the Island of Hawaii, at the world's most exclusive resort.

My wealthy mentors opened up to me a realm of fortune and adventure, in which money came alive. At the start of my apprenticeship, before the *real* work began, I floated through a state of magic bordering on bliss. Encouraged, I began play with life, taking ever-bigger risks.

One day I took the final step: I quit my job. Like a cartoon character racing off a cliff, I hovered in mid-air, legs spinning for what seemed like an eternity -- and then I dropped. Bruised and shaken, on the valley floor, I tried to put the pieces back together. I discovered that the issue I kept stumbling over wasn't really money after all.

I'd been using money as a drug, addictively, to alternately fuel and numb me to the endless task of working. I believed, on some deep level, that I had to work hard to earn everything: love, success, even salvation. Nothing in my world was unconditional or easy.

As I lay in pieces at the bottom of that cliff, I faced a

difficult choice. I was unemployed and broke. Would I go back to working, and scratch my way up the old mountain again? Or would I take this opportunity to heal?

Once upon a lonely time, I asked the lost, abandoned portions of myself to teach me what they needed. My private tutors ranged from fear to shame, from higher self to inner child, from lover to manipulator. I asked each of them to share a secret gift with me.

As I welcomed all these inner voices, and stopped judging them, something magical began to happen. I stopped working hard to prove my worth. I learned to love myself without conditions.

And the world, as it usually does, agreed with my self-image. The more I loved and supported myself, the easier it was to attract that same support from the outside world. Inspiration dropped from the sky. Opportunities knocked, often. I learned how to ask for what I wanted. Strangers volunteered to help. Money flowed.

For three years I've lived in this brand new world, abundantly, effortlessly, without "working" for a living. I do what I want, make my own schedule, change my "job description" on a whim. All I ever do is share myself and what I'm learning. I love money unconditionally, exactly as I love myself. I put no limits on the world, and it puts none on me.

As part of that unlimited reality, I embrace each stranger as another lost part of myself. I invite you into my most secret heart. I ask you to consider me no more, and no less, than another lost part of yourself, now happily found.

Imagine that, together, we can walk from fear to joy, from money dependence to lasting abundance. We can break through all the false beliefs; we can piece together all the broken dreams; we can learn to co-create a life of unconditional success.   I want to tell you how this happened for me. I want to tell you a true story about learning how to open up to life and money, infinitely, unconditionally.

To do that honestly, I must begin at the beginning.

- $ -

HITTING THE BRICK WALL

My parents' parents were at peace with money. They made do with what they had, and felt no need for more. All of them lived through World War and Great Depression. They survived; that was enough.

Grandma Paula re-used everything. When her clothes ripped or wore out, they got mended. When the dishes broke, she glued them back together. "This will do," she'd say.

Grandma shared her breakfast with the birds and squirrels. As she sipped her coffee on the back porch, she would sprinkle toast crumbs down the steps. "Man doesn't live by bread alone," she'd smile mysteriously.

She worked till she was nearly eighty, an accounting clerk at a department store, forever counting other people's money. She never wanted to retire, but her eyes were failing, and her mind began to mix the numbers. At last they had to let her go.

She couldn't fathom how to stop working. For Grandma, the purpose of the present was to build for the future. When I was younger, I imagined her putting everything she earned, from money to heavenly grace, into giant piggy banks, and hiding them under the bed. Her financial philosophy was the same as her religion: endure suffering now, your reward will come later.

From her bed she could see the steeple of her parish church, and hear its bells toll out the hours. In her heart of hearts, I think she would have liked to be a nun. She wasn't even my real grandma, but a great-aunt who had taken in my dad when his own mother died in the Depression.

She taught me, by example, the rewards of spiritual discipline. In later years, I found a soul-mate in her, even though we disagreed about religious methods. She refused to go beyond the teachings of the Church; I could scarcely be contained by them.

Nevertheless, there was a deep and mutual respect for one another, and for the progress each of us was making on our separate pathways. We both lived in the invisible realms as much as in this world of flesh, and we both knew it.

My father threw off the shackles of religion when he came of age. He moved out to a working-class suburb, and raised five little kids on a schoolteacher's salary.

Money was a constant struggle. Mostly we learned to do without, and to put value on the many great experiences money couldn't buy. Our family vacations tended to be camping trips, in a tent out by a lake or in the woods. As a special treat, Dad dressed us up in miner's hats and took us underground into the Ozark caves.

We were taught to be supportive, and to work together. Giving was expected, without recognition or reward. To get something in return, especially money, transformed the good deed into something crass. Christian charity would only count in Heaven if it wasn't cashed in now.

When I started working, I gravitated toward low-paying jobs with high emotional rewards: child-care, hospitals, social service, healing. Financially, I did without. I wanted my life to be a spiritual adventure, and money seemed like just another stupid bother.

In time, my quest for new experiences took me out on the road. My travels exposed me to other kinds of people, and I began to see that not everyone lived with the same kind of limits I accepted for myself. Some people had a lot of money; some enjoyed spending it; and not all the worthwhile things in life were free.

And so I started working harder. I switched my efforts to more lucrative fields, which brought more money, but less satisfaction.

From time to time, I splurged. Spending brought me temporary pleasure, followed by a losing struggle to catch up. I jumped aboard a creaking financial roller-coaster: spend and pay, spend and pay. Every bone-jerking ride to the top was followed by a stomach-churning plummet to the bottom.

In the midst of a particularly big-time free-fall, I spun off the track entirely. The interest on my credit cards outdistanced monthly payments; without spending a penny, I was sinking ever deeper into debt.

One night I had a conversation with an old friend who was living in Hawaii. Nicole told me that jobs were easy pickings there. I put my bills on hold, scraped some money together for a plane ticket, and left the next month.

It was not prime hiring season when I first arrived. I stayed at Nicole's place, and waited for an opening at the resort where she was working. One afternoon the phone finally rang.

It was not the resort.

My dad was on the line; his voice was brusque and choppy. Cutting through the pleasantries, he said, "Your Grandma's dying."

Finally! After ninety years of living, my beloved grandmother was ready to move on. She'd been praying for this day as long as I could remember.

And for as long as I knew how, I'd been preparing myself to help her with this transition. I'd studied death, worked with the dying, talked religion with her, spoken with doctors and angels. I was ready to hold her gnarled hand, ease it open, and coach her toward the light.

And I couldn't get to her.

I couldn't afford a plane ticket.

I was stranded on a rock in the middle of the Pacific Ocean three days later, when my grandma, shaking and confused, asked where I was, and died.

Something snapped inside of me. This time I'd lost much more than just another money battle. I was the only member of the family my grandmother trusted with matters of the soul. I'd lost my last chance on earth to help this woman who had always been there for me, who had loved me unconditionally from the day that I was born. I'd failed because I simply couldn't get my money act together.

I told Dad I was sorry, dropped the phone, and kicked the screen door open.

The beach by the house was deserted; only stars were out to keep me company. I flung myself into the surf. I screamed and threw fistfuls of sand. I cursed everything I ever knew, including the midnight sky and God.

"What do you want from me?" I shouted. "Why did you put me here? How can I do what I came here to do if I don't have the money to do it? I DON'T KNOW HOW TO LIVE LIKE THIS! I WANT OUT! GET ME OFF OF THIS MISERABLE PLANET!"

The wind howled and the ocean crashed, but no one came to carry me away. Exhausted, I collapsed on the beach, my body racked with sobs.

With snot on my face and sand in my eyes, I swore that I was through with poverty. No more limitations; no more regrets.

I vowed to master money if it killed me.

- $ -

RUSHING THE GOLD COAST

The winds from Alaska race south across 5,000 miles of open ocean before they slam into the mountains of Hawaii. Along the way, they sweep up moisture which condenses into clouds. These clouds are stopped cold by the snow-capped peak of Mauna Kea. On its northeastern slopes, in the lush highland rainforests, they dump 300 inches of water a year.

While the highlands soak, on the opposite side of the island, the Gold Coast bakes. The mountains have wrung out the clouds. Here, the skies are always blue. So much reliable sunshine on a tropical island is every vacationer's dream, but for one slight problem: the Gold Coast is a vast black-lava desert.

This problem was solved, after several million years, by ingenuity and American money. The desert bloomed in 1965, when Laurance Rockefeller piped in water from the far side of the mountain. Where Mauna Kea gently slopes into the western sea, he built his Mauna Kea Beach Hotel, the first of the Gold Coast's jet-set playgrounds. Its golf course alone drinks up a million gallons of water a day.

Hundreds of thousands of plants were imported to landscape the courtyards and grounds; the desert bloomed with fragrant frangipani and gardenia, palm trees and exotic orchids. Giant banyan trees were shipped in to shelter thousands of tropical birds, and soon the air was filled with song.

Rockefeller set the standard for Gold Coast resorts. His priceless Asian art collection was casually scattered around the hotel. Turn any corner, and a five-hundred-year-old Buddha might be staring at you. Turn again, and you might run into a Kennedy, a Vanderbilt, or European royalty. Everyone with money came to see the paradise that money built.

And so the remote and inaccessible Big Island, twice the

size of all the other Hawaiian isles combined, finally opened up to the outside world. It was new, it was different, and it was expensive.

At the center of the Gold Coast, plopped smack into the lap of luxury, was the Mauna Lani Bay Hotel. Its name meant "Mountain Reaching Heaven"; it scored the only five-diamond rating on the coast. Here Mr. Rockefeller's lessons were carried one step further. Not content with physical perfection, Mauna Lani added the elements of spiritual grace and aloha. Here in this beautiful paradise, healing peace and joy would flow into your heart like warm liquid sunshine.

My friend Nicole worked in the finest dining room at Mauna Lani. She charmed her guests with a delightful French accent that seemed to grow thicker each year. She was always eager to bless you with the chef's latest triumph, quick to argue the fine points of vintage or herb. In her native Paris, she would have been just one more pearl in a city of jewels. Here in the Pacific, far from home, she took on a more select, exotic air.

From her I learned that everything has value if you put it in the proper setting. Every gem, set off by the right contrast and color, can sparkle with originality and depth.

Soon after Grandma died, Nicole got me a job at Mauna Lani. It was part-time, and still off-season. I wasn't making much money. But I had breached the bastions of the rich, and was eager to learn.

I scoured the hotel, investigating everything, making a pest of myself. I was also making friends. I asked the maids to teach me how to make a bed, and the janitors how to care for marble floors. I haunted the kitchens, learning the names and tastes and colors of the local fish, the best imported brands of chocolate, how to whip up a souffle. Bartenders shared their secret recipes. The winemasters walked me through the subtleties of vintage and varietal. Nicole quizzed me every day, and my knowledge and confidence grew.

I learned that the qualities I'd developed in myself, through a lifetime of service to the poor and needy, could be of value to the rich as well. Enthusiasm brought a smile to everyone's face, regardless of financial status; genuine aloha was always in demand.

The native islanders moved at a languid, tropical pace as they worked; in contrast, I was a whirlwind of activity and focus. Set against their island ways, I sparkled like a jewel. As I made my rounds, caught up in my own curiosity, people in high places noticed me.

My hours at the hotel were limited, and I kept them as full as I could. Perhaps my whirlwind of activity was a defense against the helplessness I felt in my emotional and financial affairs. At least in this one aspect of my life, I could take charge and grow.

I lived a double life back then: at the hotel, I immersed myself in the lifestyles of the rich, and on my own time, I dropped back into poverty. I lived on the bleak desert hillside, outside the magic circle of the resorts. At night, I lay on my rooftop, watching the stars and thinking about money.

One of our roommates, JF, had worked with me before in California. We often talked out under those stars, about money and people and life. I helped him start a simple business on the island, cleaning cars, and nursed him through the daily ups and downs of self-employment. Both of us wanted to get beyond money, to have freedom to live and travel as we chose. Neither of us knew how.

"Why is money so confusing?" we would ask each other. "Why are there so many different opinions about how to make it? How come prosperity books don't really work? What's the problem with positive thinking?"

"You must ask the right questions to get the right answers," my father used to say. But real insights into money still remained elusive.

On my many days off, I would wander alone into the wilderness. There, in the seclusion of a canyon or an old deserted cave, I would scream myself hoarse or cry until my tears ran dry.

I had a lifetime of feelings trapped inside of me, which I'd never wanted to acknowledge. What was the point? I believed I was helpless to resolve them.

Grieving my grandmother's death brought those emotions

to the surface. That primed the pump, and soon I was flooded with rusty emotions. All the ancient feelings came, which had longed to be expressed and later died inside of me, before I ever even knew they had existed. All the stillborn children of my heart came out into the light. One by one I held each tiny body in my arms, kissed it softly, and then let the ocean carry it away.

As I flushed emotion from my body, it changed. Or maybe my perception of it changed. It felt lighter and more buoyant, as though the slightest breeze could pass through it. At the same time -- and this was another contradiction which I didn't understand -- that same body seemed more solid. I was more aware of the sensations which now registered in every pore.

As I scrambled down the hillsides, I felt every pebble under my feet; over the treetops, the sky shimmered with new shades of blue. I felt alive in ways I'd never felt before. I wandered the beaches, floated in the healing waters of the sea, soaked up the warmth of the sun.

As I released old habits of mind and heart and body, I came ever closer to a deep and peaceful emptiness. The clutter and the clatter and the chatter dropped away. And in that silence, I began exploring what I *really* knew about the world and money.

It wasn't much. Certainly not much of value.

I looked around at the people I knew, my friends of many years, the people I'd worked with and played with and loved.

Who was succeeding? Who was doing what they truly wanted to be doing with their lives? Not one of us.

Who really knew about love, with strength and passion and consistency? I could only name two.

Who was really making money? Who could work and play when they pleased? Who could buy whatever they wanted whenever they wanted it? No one I knew.

No wonder I'm not getting anywhere, I thought. Where are my teachers? I've got no examples, no support. No wonder I hold myself back! No one I know is living a life I'd want to follow. Everyone is compromising, working, struggling, fighting. Where is the love? Where is the joy and the fun?

I needed help with this, and I was not going to get it from

any of my friends.

I was in the right place at Mauna Lani. The hotel was swarming with guests who had money. Vacationers were more relaxed and open, in the island spirit, but I wasn't sure how to get close enough to ask them what I really wanted. I needed to know them intimately: how they thought and felt and acted, how they made money and spent it. I needed to be friends with them, not just another smiling face in the hallway.

I was working with the wealthy. That was a good first step. Now how could I begin to play with them?

- $ -

BUTLER TO THE RICH AND FAMOUS

"Welcome to the Bungalows." My new boss smiled at me. It was the start of the winter season, and I'd just been transferred to the most elite department in the whole resort: The Bungalows. Five private villas dropped along the sea, in a setting of incomparable beauty. Five precious jewels, with service so superb that *Lifestyles of the Rich and Famous* toasted this as "The #1 Resort in the USA." I should know: during his stay here, I was Robin Leach's private butler.

At the Bungalows, you got whatever your heart desired. Cocktails served poolside, breakfast in bed. Lessons with a tennis pro, massage beside the hot tub, a pedicure on the beach. The latest videos and CDs from our private library. Newspapers and magazines from anywhere in the world. Your choice of a new Lamborghini or a Land Rover for that little spin around the island. And the world's most glamorous neighbors, on your own secluded street of dreams.

Whatever you wanted was exactly what you got. Money was no object in the Bungalows. If you worried about price, you didn't come: the rent alone was $3,500 a night.

As your butler, I headed the household staff, and supervised the satisfaction of your every desire. I met you at the airport with a limo and champagne, and packed your luggage up when it was time to go. In between, I became your indispensable tour guide and trusted confidante.

You asked me to arrange an anniversary surprise? I trailed scented flowers from the front door to the master bedroom, lit the bungalow with candles, and laid a single silver rose upon your sweetheart's pillow. When you came back from dinner, your favorite romantic melodies were singing from the hidden speakers. The pool lights were discreetly dimmed, so you might end the evening with a starlight swim...

Now, what to do on Tuesday? How about a deep-sea fishing trip, or chartering a yacht to take a dozen friends across to Maui? We could always helicopter to secluded coves, perhaps one with a black sand beach, and leave you for an afternoon of total privacy.

For dinner? We might barbecue some lobster on the terrace at sunset, with the ocean lapping just beyond the fishponds; or serve a formal ten-course dinner in the dining room, for two guests or twelve, with polished silver, and crystal glinting in soft candlelight. Would you like hula dancers for an entertainment, or a pianist to play Rachmaninoff?

Whatever you wanted was exactly what you got. The magic was so palpable, its spell extended everywhere. Even I was not immune...

I'd finally broken through the barrier. I was rubbing elbows with the richest people on the planet, and learning firsthand how they lived and thought. From every continent the ultra-rich stopped by to play, to do business, or to rest between vacations. All of them were paying thousands of dollars a day to be with me in this island paradise, and every one of them had secrets to share.

My financial situation improved here, and so did my attitude. I soaked up luxury like a sponge, and gradually learned to relax. The split between my private world and work began to heal. Working for money was fun, for a change, and I liked that.

I also liked what I was learning about wealth and success, although I must admit it shocked me to the core. As I peeled away the endless layers of my misunderstanding, I was saddened to see that they were deeper than I'd ever imagined. Everything I'd been taught about success, until then, had been filtered through the prejudices of the unsuccessful; envy and fear colored almost all of my beliefs.

Ashamed, I began dropping assumptions and judgments about people with money. The rich weren't all monsters. Not all of them stole from the poor, mistreated their employees, or exploited the environment. Not all of them were secretly unhappy.

Some were peaceful; some shocked me with their openness and warmth. Many were more vibrant and real than my friends of a lifetime.

Chatting over after-dinner brandy, or lounging by the pool, I found my guests were often willing to include me in their conversations. In the spirit of aloha, formalities soon fell away. I played on the floor with their children, ran into the marble bathroom with another towel or a drink. We learned to trust one another, to relax together.

Most of my guests were naturally curious, and they wondered about living on the island. They asked about my life, how I came to the Bungalows, what my dreams were for the future.

Some were merely making conversation, but others offered friendship of the heart. With them, I shared confidences, reflecting on life and love and money. I felt as easy with them as I have with poorer friends in poorer places, when we'd talked on porch steps in the cool air of a summer evening, or dawdled over cups of coffee in an all-night diner.

After awhile I got my courage up, and started asking questions of my own. What was it like to be wealthy? How did one make a great deal of money? What were the secrets of success?

Their answers surprised me. I wrote many of them down, wanting to remember them, determined to put them into practice for myself. At the time, I thought I understood what they were saying.

I knew nothing. Only later did these seeds begin to crack and sprout and truly blossom. After I left the magic circle of the Bungalows, the full impact of all these words dawned in my body, and I became aligned with money in a way I never knew was possible.

But first, I had to learn a different way to think about success. My teachers helped me pry the bars off my prison cell; they led me from a world of limitation into one of endless energy and life.

- $ -

THE LAST TABOO

"Why is it so awkward for people to talk about money?" I asked an influential European psychiatrist early on in my stay at the Bungalows. He was smoking an after-dinner cigar on the terrace while his wife put the children to bed.

"I don't mean money in general: everyone has opinions about the economy. A lot of people are willing to share business strategies, or to brag about successful investments. But nobody wants to say what they're worth. If I ask about personal income, suddenly the conversation stops cold. Why is that such a big deal?"

"Money is the last taboo," he said, conspiratorially. The tip of his cigar glowed in the darkness.

I shifted my weight. The terrace flagstones were hard on my feet. The psychiatrist, a rather obnoxious man in his sixties, leaned back in his comfortable chair. Although he was enjoying this family vacation, I could tell he missed a certain level of stimulating conversation, and also -- if the truth be told -- a certain sense of self-importance. Over the last few days my naivete and eagerness to learn had brought out the teacher in him, a role he seemed to relish.

His generosity came partly from the fact that he was staying in the Bungalows for free. Sometimes businesses would book conventions in the hotel and provide bungalow accommodations as a perk to their CEOs and, occasionally, their distinguished guest speakers. I met Ronald Reagan and a number of other luminaries under just those circumstances. Mr. Reagan, by the way, was willing to recite generic parables about success, but declined my invitation to share more personal secrets.

"How taboo is money?"

My private lecturer sipped on the coffee I had set before

him, and launched into another speech. "Listen to the very words we use: filthy rich, filthy lucre, the idle rich, the almighty dollar, making a killing in the market. We tell our children to wash their hands after touching it, to keep it out of their mouths. The prejudice runs so deep it's almost unconscious.

"In our society, money is the last taboo. Wealth is as socially unacceptable as poverty; they both create their own brands of discomfort. As much as we glorify money, we fear it. Money has symbolic power over us.

"Look at how we treat the poor and homeless. In other societies, they are accepted; no one begrudges a beggar his begging. Here, they are shamed. We believe there's something personally wrong with them. Subconsciously, if we can blame them for their circumstances, make them responsible for their poverty, then we can distance ourselves from their misery. In America, poverty comes from character defects, not flaws in the economic system. So being poor is socially unacceptable.

"Wealth is also socially taboo. The rich are subtly shamed for their wealth. Some of them even do it to themselves! Believe it or not, the rich feel guilty, too. Many of my clients complain that money is a problem for them. Especially inherited money. More than a century ago, Honore de Balzac summed up the popular notion: 'Behind every great fortune there is a great crime.' The children of the rich are often ashamed they haven't earned their wealth themselves, or afraid that the family fortune is tainted because Uncle Albert exploited his workers.

"Money separates them from the mass of humanity. It's hard to tell who's your friend, and who's a fortune-hunter; who loves you for yourself, and who's only gold-digging. Wealth isolates. Many of the rich feel trapped inside their social class, often with people they don't much care for. It becomes difficult to trust anyone who isn't just as rich as you. Sometimes it's even dangerous. For always, where there is money, there are those who would steal it.

"This situation is unique to humans. It is at the root of the taboo. In the animal kingdom, status and power are clear. In the jungle, you can easily see who has the biggest penis or the greatest strength. Power can be challenged, with bared teeth or clashing horns, but never stolen.

"In civilization, personal power's not so obvious. We live in a more abstract world. Physical size and strength are not as important to us in our mating and leadership rituals. Because we can't tell at a glance who's superior, we have to measure status with secondary objects: the success of our businesses, the size of our houses and cars, the cut of our clothes, the beauty of our women."

I cringed at that last remark. This aging scholar had a trophy wife, half his age and twice as pretty. I wasn't sure how she felt about their marriage or his blatant sexism, and I wasn't about to ask. She was uncomfortably close to my own age. We skated around each other warily, avoiding all close contact. As a waiter, I'd learned long ago not to flirt with the girl when her date would be leaving your tip.

"There's a lot more room to maneuver when income is only hinted at," the guy who would be leaving my tip continued. "It's like a poker game where everybody's bluffing."

"Why would anyone need to bluff if they really have money?" I jumped back in the conversation.

"Because they're all insecure about their money," he replied with an expansive grin. "That's the base of the taboo.

"Money's not a part of you, like claws or teeth. It's something separate, which you acquire. The animals have it easy: their power is built in; it's what they are. They don't carry their strength in a wallet, or borrow it from a bank.

"Because your money isn't an essential part of you, like muscles or size, it can be stolen or lost. Your businesses can be bought and sold; your houses can burn down. All the civilized measures of power can be taken away: possessions, positions, even reputations. They're all secondary. They're all fragile. That makes man the only animal that knows insecurity."

Something dawned on me. "Is that why wealth is so often kept hidden?"

"Invariably," he replied. "Old money is usually discreet, like mafioso who carry pistols but rarely use them. The power is simply understood. Only the nouveau riche flaunt their wealth."

I certainly agreed with that. The most conspicuous consumers I had met at the Bungalows were all people who had made their own money, who had come up from nothing and succeeded. They flashed jewelry, dropped hundred-dollar bills on every doorman and bellboy, yapped on and on about their villas and vacations.

The people who were born into wealth were invariably quiet, dignified, and simple. They weren't trendy in their clothing or their meals. They rarely made a fuss. They had simple standards: as long as everything was done to perfection, they were happy.

My lecturer's wife came out of the bungalow and stood behind her husband. I shifted from one foot to the other, suddenly feeling uncomfortable. "Perhaps I should take in these dishes?" I inquired. "Or bring a coffee for your wife?"

He waved at me impatiently. "No, no, I'm rather enjoying this. Sandra, do sit down. Are you finished with the children?"

"They're both asleep," she yawned. "Maybe I do need some coffee."

"Finish this," he pushed his cup across the table toward her, waving me back. "Now, where were we? Ah, yes. Money and taboos. Socially, the topic of income is considered vulgar, because it's impolite to expose each other's insecurities. We pretend that money simply doesn't matter. Of course this desire to be discreet is matched by an equal desire to brag, and thus is born hypocrisy.

"We go to great lengths to prove our worth to each other without ever actually mentioning dollars and cents. Hence the businesses and titles, the art collections and yachts, all the paraphernalia of wealth. The human equivalent of arched backs and ruffled feathers and all that huffing and puffing that birds and frogs do in the wild.

"In American society, these questions of status get very confusing. The old lines used to be drawn by class, and not very long ago, those lines were etched in stone. Rare was the bird who flew over them. Nowadays, the lines are still there, but they're much less barriers than simple distinctions.

"There is movement from one class to another, though not so frequent as the cinemas or lotteries would have you believe. In general, the rich stay rich and the poor stay poor. The bulk of each class never changes. The circumstances of birth are difficult to overcome.

"Each of us is born to certain advantages and disadvantages, both material and psychological. The poor are taught to be poor, and inherit few financial resources to change their lot. The rich are taught to be rich, and receive the tools and wherewithal to carry on the task of making fortunes.

"Those early patterns can be broken only with great diligence, and the guidance of professionals. Alas, our services prove too expensive for the lower classes..."

A breeze came up over the ocean as the moon broke through a rack of clouds. His wife shivered momentarily. I felt overwhelmed that she and I should be privileged to experience such great luxury, and sad for what it cost us. She had to marry this man to get into that world, and I had to work as a servant.

"Is there no other way?" I protested.

He left me with a final set of keys. "Studies show that there are six common factors in those who rise above their lot to make a fortune. All of them have goals, most clearly written. Many are highly educated. Most are ambitious and work hard: it's not uncommon for a self-made millionaire to work for eighty-plus hours a week. Some believe it's who you know, and aim to move in the right circles. Most are risk takers; the greatest rewards usually require the greatest risks. And with tax structures what they are, personal ownership of a corporation is crucial to acquiring significant wealth."

Goals. Education. Hard work. The right circles. Risk taking. Creating corporations. I tried to remember them all.

I excused myself by saying it was late, that I should leave them to enjoy their privacy. He swallowed the bait. The smell of brandy and cigar smoke trailed behind them as he led his prize in through the arching bougainvillea to bed.

- $ -

SLAVES TO MONEY

"Was it always like this?" I wondered. "Were rich and poor always so hopelessly divided?"

I was telling the pool boy about my conversation with the psychiatrist. An avid surfer, Bok had traveled from Australia in search of waves, and landed here for "just a season, till I build the funds back up." I'd often heard him on the local beaches, arguing with native activists. He seemed to know a lot about politics, and I figured he could fill me in on history.

"Oh yeah, mate," he replied, skimming a few petals from the center of the pool. "There have always been the wealthy and the poor, as long as there's been civilization. At least, so far as we know: history itself is little more than what the victors tell us. The blokes in power, the people with the money, make the records. The stories of the poor die with them, and are buried out back in their unmarked graves. Whoever wins, writes the history; the poor and disenfranchised have no voice."

"I never thought of it that way."

"You're not supposed to, mate. That's the plan. And it's a long and glorious plan, stretching back for millennia. The history of wealth begins with violence, moves through war to politics, and ends with slavery."

"Oh, come on, Bok! We're obviously not slaves; we can come and go as we please."

"Oh, can we really? Could you walk out on this job today?"

"No one could stop me."

"Don't be silly. You're still trapped; the cage is only one size bigger than it used to be. You'd trade one master for another; nothing else would change. Our chains are economic, social, psychological. They don't need whips and metal cuffs today.

"In most places, at most times, the wealthy have used violence and force to hold onto their power. Kings built castles which could be defended. Every penny-ante drug lord has a private militia; even the Pope has an armed guard.

"Those in power nowadays have found an easier way to keep the slaves from revolting: the myth of upward mobility. We're all promised a place at the banquet table, if we work hard or get lucky. In this new fairy tale, we can all live like kings!

"Upward mobility is a subversively dangerous belief. It trumpets that the walls between the rich and poor have tumbled down, that there's no barrier between the workers and the wealth. Anyone can make it in America! Did you know eighty percent of this country's millionaires were born poor?

"That sounds great until you look at a few other stats: for instance, that twenty percent of the population controls eighty percent of the nation's wealth. And how about the great public robbery of the 1980's? In the late 1970's, the richest one percent of the people owned twenty percent of the wealth; by 1989, their share had risen to nearly forty percent. One percent of the people own forty percent of the wealth!

"They take the very wealth they used to hide behind their barricades, and flaunt it on TV for all to see. People don't revolt now at inequities; they envy and lust, they want it for themselves. Seeing pictures of it makes them drool, and forget about taking any righteous social action. Don't work to change the system; work to win its power for yourself!"

He shook his head in scorn. "And we participate in this charade, mate. Every day, we polish the boots of the masters." He shook out his pool net, and scooped up the flowers he had gathered. "We're working in its biggest temple here," he cast an eye around the Bungalow compound.

"We let in Robin Leach with TV cameras, to go on and on about the people who have made the leap to fame and fortune. They glamourize the show of wealth, and on the way, use us to keep the fairy-tale machine well-lubricated. We're puppets, mate. You and I are bloody dog biscuits, waved before the noses of the middle class, to keep the poor sods working. We're part of the reward for those who make it! 'A fabulous Bungalow, with your own private pool boy and butler...'"

He packed up his gear and turned to leave. With a wink, he added, "Someday when we have the time, I'll tell you why these Bungalows are really here. That's a story that will curl your socks, mate. Later!" And with that, he was off.

- $ -

KING OF THE CAVEMEN

I know now that the world reflects whatever you believe about it. You'll get only what you think is possible. Back when I started at the Bungalows, I was too innocent to see that clearly.

I thought I was discovering, for the first time in my life, what the real world was made of. *Au contraire*, as Nicole would have said. I was merely seeing, in the flesh, the vivid outlines of my own buried prejudice and fear.

"Get me a beer, boy!" My next guest, a burly man in his sixties, shouted through the dark at me. He'd instructed me to keep the shutters closed, night and day. From my position near the wall, I could catch a sliver of terrace and the glare off the water. It was "too damn hot" out in the sun, so I was serving lunch inside to my guest and a visitor.

For once I was glad to have my tuxedo jacket on. The air conditioner was set at sixty, and that, combined with the darkness, made the bungalow seem like a cave. After I'd delivered another Heineken, I slipped back into the shadows of the dining room, staring absently out into space.

My guest banged his fist on the table. "Money goes to the strongest," he shouted. The word *money* brought me back, and I decided to eavesdrop. This man would never bother to have a conversation with me; in fact, he barely acknowledged my presence. I still wanted to know how he created money.

"You know the way it works," he continued. "You got the drive? You got the stamina? Don't waste your time with small-time ideas and two-bit operations. Jeez, how can you even consider working with those guys?"

He snorted with disgust, and dug into his plate of barbecued ribs. Without apology to anyone, he still ate and drank and swore like a trucker. Somehow he'd built a major transportation network, with trucking lines from one coast to the other, and cargo ships to back them up. His empire had made him a millionaire many times over.

His visitor was twenty years younger, and slightly slicker, but they both looked like they would have been at home on any Brooklyn bowling team. They were apparently discussing some business project.

"There's nothing secret or mysterious about it, Jerry," the older man explained. "The guy with the biggest guns wins. Always has, always will."

"But Joe, you gotta plan for the future sometime. Maybe biggest won't always be best. What's gonna happen when Dallas starts shipping by rail?"

"It'll never happen. Too many big boys got a piece of the action. Don't worry, they'll protect their investments." He called for another beer.

"But what am I gonna do with all that land?"

"Jeez, land is land. Keep it. You can always use it later. The old man used to tell me all the time: land, land, land. It's the one investment that will never fail." He grabbed his glass, and pounded it on the table. "Get something solid, something REAL, for Christ's sake. Put a lid on your hare-brained ideas. Trends are a dime a dozen, they come and go. All the fancy stuff and fancy talk will blow away, but land and warehouses and trucks, now that's something real. Something you can lay your hands on."

"Don't bet the farm on it, Joe. Some things are changing fast."

"Listen, I've seen it all come and go. Any way you slice it, people gotta eat, they gotta live in houses and drive to work and put clothes on their backs and feed the kids. They'll always need the basics: food and bricks and lumber and cars. Why take chances on the rest? With this project, this Henderson thing, you're takin' unnecessary risks. Stick with the land, Joe. Stick with what you got. It's a safe bet."

"Even after the factories all close and move down to Mexico?"

"Let 'em move to Mexico! The farther they go, the more I stand to make. Somebody's gotta ship it back to market. Christ, we can get it coming and going! You gotta roll with the punches, know what I mean? Too much planning don't always pan out."

"Who's gonna have any money to spend if nobody's working?"

"I keep telling you, it's only temporary. You gotta take the long picture, Jerry. Trust the big boys. They're not gonna let the whole economy fall apart. Sure, they shave off their cut, but they know you can't bleed a rock. It might get close to the bone, but they ain't gonna let the whole damn system die. Guaranteed."

"I think you overestimate those guys. They got the Japanese breathing down their necks, and Hong Kong and Germany and who-the-hell-knows who else. It's not the same world you grew up in."

"So the pot gets bigger: business is still business. The boys at the top will hold it together, I don't care if they're yellow or red or green. Money is power. Money calls the shots. Now, for me, all I gotta do is move the little pieces from one place to another. Plenty of work in that. Plenty of little pieces to move. Always was, always will be.

"If you know what's good for you, you'll just slow down and work a simple angle, too. Not your wild-eyed rabbit shit about what's coming down the road. Something real and solid, something you can bank on. Let the college boys win and lose their shirts playing with a bunch of made-up numbers. We'll outlast 'em all."

"Well, you're in a slightly better position to say that than me."

"You're sitting on land. What more do you need? Stick with the basics. Come hell or high water, people need to eat, and have a roof over their heads. They need a little land to farm or put a house on, or a factory, or a strip mall. Or a golf course like this one, for Christ's sake! The rest is bullshit speculation. Don't second-guess history, kid. The big ideas come and go. Stick with the basics."

"I don't know, Joe. I got burned on that last deal real bad.

Held my cards too long. History don't always repeat itself. Maybe things are really changing this time."

"What am I gonna do with you?" The shipping magnate shrugged his shoulders and flapped his hands in the air. "You wear me out with your God-damn questions and your trumped-up theories. Who's been feeding you that crap? What you need's another drink. Hey, you!" he shouted over to me. "More beers."

When I got back from the kitchen, they had finished. The transportation king was sacked out on the sofa watching ESPN. His visitor was in the john. I laid down two more beers, and left them sitting in the dark.

- $ -

KEEPER OF THE SECRETS

That evening I had some thinking to do. I went for a walk on the beach just after sunset. By the light of a half-moon, I walked through my reactions to the day.

I had always hated men like this; it was a shock to see them in the flesh. They were the reason I avoided money, especially in its relationship to power. There was something dark and cold and dense about the realms they moved in. Being with them gave me chills.

Those chills were often interrupted with flashes of anger. Not because they were abusing me, but because they were ignoring me. Someone like me was irrelevant in their dense and solid world. For them, I didn't even exist. I was neither threat nor ally, friend nor foe. In the equations of power, I didn't even count.

The qualities I valued, from intellect to heart and soul, were of no use to them at all. They wouldn't recognize a feeling or a fresh idea if it smacked them in the face. We had no common ground on which to meet, nothing to say to one another beyond "More beer," and "Here you go, sir."

I realized that I discounted them as much as they discounted me. It was so tempting to believe that they were evil! Once or twice, I got beyond my anger and felt a twinge of compassion, but I couldn't make it last. I still hated everything they stood for.

For a while, I despaired of ever learning anything from them. They shut me out, and I in turn refused to let them in. What good could possibly come from this stalemate? We'd drawn the boundary lines between us, and now we were stuck defending them. How could I ever make money if I refused to participate in their very physical and focused world?

I wrestled with the issue of power for the next few weeks.

Then one night, I was talking with Leilani, an older woman who taught hula classes at the resort. We got into a conversation about local land developers. I shared my feelings about men who value violence and power. She disagreed with me, and said there was someone I needed to meet, a very old kahuna who understood the real secrets of power.

A kahuna is a Hawaiian holy man, often skilled in the arts of healing, who passes on the wisdom of the ancestors. Part doctor, part spiritual technician, in other cultures he might be called a medicine man or a shaman. To Hawaiians, the name *kahuna* literally means "keeper of the secrets." I was very privileged that Leilani agreed to introduce me; usually foreigners were not invited to the native rituals.

On the day we were to go, Leilani picked me up. We chatted as she drove up through the pass toward the wet side of the island. I was just a little nervous.

In a tiny village near the coast, we pulled to a stop before a weather-beaten shack with a rusted tin roof. A wiry, gap-toothed old man came out to greet us. He was dressed in western clothes, with a cowboy hat a size too big. Leilani presented him a bag full of mangoes, and in we went.

The two of them spoke for a while in Hawaiian. I couldn't understand most of what they said, and my focus drifted to the rain drumming on the roof. When I let go of trying to follow their individual words, I began to hear the language as a melody, and soon it joined the rain to make a song. Suddenly, I realized with a shock that I could understand it on a deeper level. All of their emotions and meanings came through in the music of their voices.

Leilani was telling a story about darkness and me. Her voice filled with sadness and unresolved questions; her words sank like heavy stones into a bottomless sea. The old man kept nodding his head and peering over in my direction, though he never looked directly at me. He seemed to be staring over my shoulder at something. His voice, when he spoke, was forceful and strong.

Then, abruptly, he ended their conversation. With gestures he commanded me to lay on a pallet at the back of the house, near the burning wood stove. He took off his hat, and sat on a chair beside me. Leilani he sent off on some errand. She returned a few minutes later with a bundle of freshly-picked ti leaves.

After a few minutes of quietly sitting, he picked up the ti leaves and began to chant. He shook them over my body, scattering cool drops of rainwater. Then he gently beat me with the leaves, from the bottom of my feet to the top of my head. At first I was startled, but soon I relaxed. The beating was soothing and rhythmic, in time with his voice. He fanned the air above me, then repeated the entire procedure twice. Leilani sat in the corner near the door, with her eyes averted.

When he'd finished, he tied the ti leaves in a bundle and dropped them into the fire. The heavy smoke gave off a most peculiar odor. I was trying to place the smell when he reached over and closed my eyes. On top of them he placed two smooth, flat stones. For the first time in this ceremony, I felt fear.

What happened next is hard to describe. I couldn't see, but I could feel him moving all around me, almost dancing, breathing heavily. I felt him lifting something out of the pit of my stomach, although he never touched my body with his hands. All the while he chanted and sang.

His song was filled with a natural power and strength. In the darkness I imagined him young and sleek, like a great fish or a jungle cat. He kept lifting the heaviness out of me, patiently and methodically, using his voice as a lever. He never seemed to strain or rush. I imagined the heaviness in me as rocks, and his singing as a work song. With each verse another rock was lifted. Eventually he had piled a great wall all around me.

"A warrior wears his armor on the outside, to protect himself," he said to me in English. "You have carried yours inside you, like a curse. What is this shame I see in young men today? They deny their warrior-nature, and live like women.

"Leilani here, has brought me several men like you, all young men of my people. You are the first *haole*, but the problem is the same. The chain has been broken, what my great-grandfathers handed down to their sons, and my father passed to me. The warrior-nature has not hardened in you. You are soft and gentle, like a woman. You hide your maleness deep inside. It is a burden for you there, instead of a great power and a gift.

"I have seen your fathers and grandfathers, the old men of your *haole* people. They are not soft; they conquer and destroy. They beat my people and steal the land of the *aumakua* and gods who have always lived here. They are powerful and strong.

"Why have they neglected to train their sons in the art of war? Why have they handed their male sons over to the women, to be raised in woman-ways? This I do not understand. It is the way of the conqueror to beat my people into slavery. That I understand. But is this happening now to the conqueror's own children? These men are surely insane. What warrior would not pass his secrets down to his own sons?"

Tears trickled out from underneath the smooth flat stones.

I'm not sure if our fathers neglected to pass on to us the ways of male energy. Perhaps they tried, and we rebelled. We saw where patriarchy led: to war without honor, to cavalier racism, to economic rape. My generation has rarely seen male power used in positive ways. The little bully throwing a tantrum grows up into the businessman who wrecks communities, destroys environments, and ruins lives.

Or is that only what the women have taught us while their husbands were away?

I tried to connect these ideas in my head, to formulate an answer to this man who seemed at peace with his own power, who shared healing energies and not destructive lies. Then I felt him tugging at the air around my face, and all ideas fell away. I could hardly put two thoughts together. There was a smoldering emptiness where my mind used to be.

In that new darkness, I felt him lifting the stones from my eyes, and pulling me up from the pallet. He led me outside into the rain, and pushed me down onto my knees. "Lay!" he commanded, and I fell face down onto the earth. "Now let the woman in you go back into the great mother. Open up your guts" -- here he kicked at my lower back with his foot -- "and spill those woman-spells back into earth." I lurched, and felt something opening inside of me. A thick black liquid poured through my navel and drained into the mud. I felt nauseous, and my head began to spin.

"Now breathe!" he shouted. "Give your putrid breath back to the earth! Push it out." He pushed on my lungs in a steady rhythm. "Huh! Huh! Huh! Huh! Huh!" we exhaled together. After several minutes my breathing slowed, and he stopped pushing me.

I was soaked, with rain or sweat, I'm not sure what. I felt light and exhilarated and exhausted.

"It's not easy working with you *haoles*," he explained to me. "I do not know your ancestors or gods. Perhaps you don't know them yourself. I do not see them close around you. Lucky for you today that mine were willing to help me with this. They tell me you belong here, too. That I do not understand. But they know more about these things than me."

He helped me up. I was covered with mud. With a strange gesture of tenderness and concentration, he smeared the mud across my face in streaks, and up into my hair. While looking at me sideways, he broke into a grin, as though he'd just now recognized me. He spoke something in Hawaiian to the air behind him, and laughed, like he was talking with some private god. I suddenly felt a chill; it seemed that every shadow was alive.

These shadow-beings were real for him, I realized. He lived in a world thick with friends and enemies, all close at hand, all invisible to me. Each was a distinct person, some more powerful than others, but all together making up a family that stretched back through time into the distant past. These gods were his ancestors, his grandfathers, the friends who had passed on. They had their own names and faces.

The white man's gods seem so abstract compared to his! We worship money, and power, and progress, and vague concepts like liberty and justice. Our gods force us to approach them mentally, because they all come from the realms of mind. There is nothing personal about them, no blood relationship, no joy.

He spoke with his gods like I would speak to Uncle Jake at a family picnic, or Cousin Bob who runs the local bank where I'm applying for a loan. They all had faces, and feelings, and personalities. Likes and dislikes. Humanity.

The more I try to be close to the white man's gods, the farther I get from myself. I lift myself above the human level, and into the realm of abstraction. Maybe this is why our system creates such abuse: the holier we get, the more powerful, the closer to success, then the farther we drift from our families and our own sense of humanity.

At that moment, I felt a connection to him and his world much more solid than anything I'd experienced at the Bungalows. Aloha was not some vague concept of love and good-will; it was a living presence, as close as breathing, as intimate as blood. I thanked him over and over. He cut me short. "It is not me you want to thank, but my *aumakua* and *ohana*, my ancestors and family. They are pleased to meet you, young man. They are pleased that you can feel their presence. This is rare in a *haole*."

He called Leilani out of the house, and spoke with her again in their native tongue. He seemed genuinely happy about what had occurred. She thanked him, and moved toward the car. He told her to take me down to the ocean to wash away the mud. I heard him use the phrase "*pi kai*."

Leilani waited while he ran inside the house for something. I asked her about *pi kai*, and she told me that it was a ceremonial purification. The ocean would cleanse away more than mud, she said. I must have seemed shaky, because she came around to help me into the car.

The kahuna man returned from his shack, and ceremoniously handed me the stones he had placed on my eyelids. "Keep these and remember always to see," he told me. "The invisible world holds just as much power as what you can see with your eyes. When you find your warrior side, remember that." I held those stones tightly all the way down the mountain to the beach.

A BREATH OF ALOHA

Leilani lived in two worlds, the modern and the world of her ancestors. She had great respect for the Hawaiian traditions, and had mastered many of the ancient practices. She spoke Hawaiian fluently, taught hula classes, and often danced herself in the resorts around the island. Many of the older Hawaiians refused to have anything to do with the exploiting economy of the whites. She, on the other hand, gracefully accepted everyone.

Her personal spiritual journey had taken her beyond the closed circle and superstitions of her people, and into a much wider sense of living. She considered herself a part of every family, and refused to limit herself to one way of life. Because of her great aloha and respect, she was accepted everywhere on the island.

"Everyone has their gift to share with us, and it is our responsibility to choose the gift which fits our need at each moment," she once told me. "I would not call a kahuna to birth my baby, nor would I call a carpenter to bury the dead. Hawaii is a land of many people now, and it is my place to share my aloha with them all. I do not know why this is so, and yet it is. I have had to grow and stretch in my loving, and this has brought me much pain and joy."

After our visit to the old kahuna, she drove me down to a beach on the east side of the island. It was gray and rainy, but I went into the ocean anyway. She left me alone for a long time, lost in my own private feelings and thoughts. When I was ready to be with company again, she walked out of the trees and invited me to come for dinner.

We drove in silence to her little cabin on the mountain. She prepared the meal, while I played with the fire. It was a relief to be with someone without socializing, and I thanked her for that gift.

After dinner, I felt ready to talk. I was still too close to my experience of the day to speak about that, but I was curious about Leilani. We had played together on several occasions with mutual friends, and chatted over potluck after some of her classes, but I had never spent any length of time alone with her.

I asked her how she balanced the worlds of the white man and her ancestors. She replied that both worlds were like different songs, and what held them together was deeper than either: it was the spirit of the music, the singer who spins both songs into being.

"I honor all people for what they are," Leilani said. "We are much closer than we pretend. These families we are born from, the cultures and peoples we embrace as uniquely our own: these are but wonderful illusions. You and I are as close as my mother and me. All people are made of the same thoughts and feelings.

"We're none of us real," she continued, gesturing out toward the falling rain. "Our feelings and our moods shift like the weather, and just as mysteriously. Thoughts come to us, we know not where from, and they circle through our minds like buzzing insects. These same thoughts and feelings come to many minds and bodies all at once. When a cloud passes over the sun, everyone out on the beach begins to shiver. So it is with all these emotions and ideas which we think are so private, which we believe to be uniquely ours."

She took down a kettle from a hook in the rafters, and set it on a windowsill to catch the falling rain. "We take these random memories and feelings, stirred by the wind, and shape them into an identity. This is who I am, we say.

"We embrace half of our thoughts, and send the others off to hell. We choose some feelings, some moods, and call them back to us, over and over. Others we ignore. The trees may be bursting with life, and all the birds in heaven singing, yet still we hang on to the same old emotions, the same old stale thoughts. Eventually we weave them into something consistent, and show it proudly to our friends and family: this is me, we say, this is who I am.

"They accept the mask we show them. Secretly, they hope that we, in turn, will accept the mask they show to us. People who wear masks fear two things only: first, will I fit in? will they accept me? and second, will I be unmasked? will everyone discover that I am a fraud?

"It is a mutual agreement that we come to, that is all. None of it is real. The ever-changing thoughts and feelings do not disappear. The outlawed emotions keep coming, the beliefs we push away refuse to disappear. We carry them deep in our bodies; often others see them before we do ourselves.

"Someone who does not care who you think you are -- an enemy, a sorcerer -- will see right through you, and read the story in your eyes, in your walk, in the lines on your face or your palm. A child will see through your pretendings, an animal will smell what you carry in your heart." She set the kettle in the fire, and reached for her basket of herbs.

I was spellbound. "Do you mean that I may not be who I say I am?"

"You *cannot* say who you are, my child. None of us ever can. I can tell you what I feel and think this moment, but the moment that I speak it, I will change. Once I see it, once I say it, it is gone..."

"How can this be?"

"Because we are alive. The nature of life is to change, to always be in motion. When change ceases, life ceases. He who does not change is a phantom, dead. Only the dead do not change." She swept the lid off the kettle, and dropped in a handful of herbs. In the firelight her skin glowed orange and gold. At the temples, streaks of silver lit her thick black hair.

"The Hawaiians saw that the white men were dead. *Haole*, they called them. Lacking-breath. They did not breathe, their spirits did not change or flow. Breath did not move in their bodies like the breathing wind moves through the body of the world. They never invited the great world to live inside their bodies, and so they were dead." She spoke slowly, almost sadly.

"What about me? I am *haole*!"

"No, my friend, you are not *haole*. It is not really a race, but a way of living. Your skin is white, but you breathe and you live in your body. If you were *haole*, I would not be speaking to you of such things. There would be no spaces in you for my words to penetrate. A *haole* is heavy and full, like a log that has lived too long in the sea. *Haoles* are full of themselves, full of old ideas, full of feelings that don't move."

I thought of all the heaviness that the kahuna had lifted out of me. I wasn't sure how to wear it on the outside, like an armor, or if I even wanted to. I just knew that he had stumbled onto something true. I felt lighter for remembering.

Leilani poured us tea. We sipped in silence for a while. The rain dripped from the trees.

Then, abruptly, she began again. "I know what *haole* is," she said, as though she were about to tell a secret. "My grandfather was *haole*."

I looked at her face for signs of what she said. Her nose seemed thinner, her eyes a bit wider. Something solid shifted, I acknowledged a kinship I had felt without understanding.

"Once, long ago, I went to the mainland to visit him, when he lay dying. My mother took me on a boat with her. I was young, not yet married, in my teens.

"My grandfather had asked us to come. In his old age, he wanted the two sides of his family to meet. His own *haole* wife was gone, the one he'd married when he returned to the mainland. All he had left were his children: my mother and her two half-brothers.

"We stayed at the house of my uncle and aunt; we lived with them for several weeks, before grandfather finally died. They had three children of their own. I played with my cousins every afternoon while the grown-ups went to the hospital.

"It was there that I discovered what *haole* really meant. My youngest cousin, the baby, was three: he still had the spark of life in him. The other two went to school every day. The oldest boy was ten. Already they had killed his soul: his eyes had no life, he acted like a little grown-up. He was mean and hateful to me and my mother.

"Margaret, the only girl, was still in kindergarten. The

strain was beginning to show on her. Her spirit was wilting, like a plant that needed water. When we'd play together, she would loosen up and start to breathe; but near her brother or her mother, she would stiffen. They were always telling her to be a good girl. God knows what they thought of me."

I could picture Leilani as a little girl quite easily. Her eyes were always open wide with the wonder of living, and she would say the most outrageous things, matter-of-factly, like a child does.

"I know what you mean about children, Leilani. I notice that about my guests. The little ones attract me, the ones who can't cut up their sandwiches yet, the ones we have to watch around the pool. The toddlers love me. It's the older ones who get snotty sometimes, and try to boss me around."

Leilani nodded. "It's a horrible crime what *haoles* do to their children," she sighed. "But they can't help it. You can't give to others what you don't have yourself."

"What do you mean?" I asked. "What don't they have?"

"They lack breath, they aren't real. Their spirits are locked in a prison of fear. 'Do it this way; don't do that; I told you *No!*; sit up straight; put your hands on your lap.' They train their children to act like the dead. It's the only way they know.

"You can't blame them, really. We pass on the gifts we've been given. The *haoles* have been taught to strangle spirit, to slowly bind their children's souls, just as the Chinese used to bind their women's feet. It is their way. I've seen it over and over. No one *listens* to children, no one follows them into the garden of joy. They're constantly yanked back into the dead world of adults, like puppets on a string. In time, they stop trying to move their own limbs. They stop breathing. Then the adults are satisfied. Not happy, mind you: that emotion is beyond their reach. But they are satisfied. No one is laughing in the corner to remind them of what they've lost."

A lone tear rolled down the side of my nose and dropped to the floor. I remembered my own childhood, my parents, school. How much my parents loved me! And yet how little of that love got through... I've always felt the love between us as a distant river, buried underground; it flows between us, but it never surfaces. The limestone walls contain it. I can hear it roaring down there in the dark, and I know that they can hear it, too. What's sad is that we don't know how to reach it, how to splash in its healing waters, how to fish in its nurturing depths.

Leilani stopped talking. She closed her eyes and gently hummed an old Hawaiian song. We sat by the firelight and rocked back and forth, slowly, as the rain ran in rivers off the roof.

I slept with Leilani that night, curled up like a baby in her arms.

- $ -

MAKING LOVE FOR MONEY

One of my favorite bits of Bungalow magic was to pick my guests out of the crowd at the airport. This never failed to impress. Not everyone who stayed with us was famous, or had a face that you would recognize. Some were smart enough to just be rich, avoiding all the hassles of celebrity and fame.

Usually our office managed to gather quite a bit of detailed information about incoming guests from their staff or travel agents, often down to their favorite beverages and sleeping habits. Sometimes we even scored biographies or photos.

With Kim and Peter, that was not the case. All I knew was their home address and the fact that they were middle-aged and married.

At the airport, I was looking for a tasteful, tailored couple from Chicago, probably bored with one another, and irritated with the lack of first class on the island-hopping aircraft. No such people came off the plane.

Sporting cheap plastic leis, and laughing hysterically, they slipped right by me without even arousing my suspicion.

Kim and Peter were loud and flashy and fun. They were also very much in love. The only time they were apart was for a few hours every morning: he played an early nine holes of golf with friends who were staying at the hotel, while she slept in. Every morning after she got up, she would lounge in the hot tub and pool, brassy blonde hair pulled back, bosoms spilling out of her bikini top, and diamonds glittering everywhere.

She and I would often talk away the time until her husband returned. On our second-to-last morning together, she wanted a bottle of Dom Perignon to mix with the orange juice I'd squeezed for breakfast. She, of course, insisted that I join her for a leisurely mimosa.

One mimosa led to another, and soon she'd finished breakfast and retired to the jacuzzi. I kept the temperature at 82 degrees because she liked "the bubbles, not the heat." The bubbles swirled madly away.

We'd been dishing dirt for awhile before I brought the conversation round to money. I asked her what her secret was. She froze, and looked at me as though she might at any moment decide that I was some long-lost lover. I felt her searching my face for more clues.

I repeated my question. "What's been your secret for making money all these years?"

"Money's easy, darlin'. It comes from the same place as love." She flashed a smile at me, and waved her diamond-covered fingers. "Or do I mean sex?" She leaned back in the jacuzzi, and laughed. I pulled the champagne bottle from the iced silver bucket, and topped off her glass.

"I found out the secret of money a long long time ago. Now it pours in so fast, I just get out of its way."

"I'd say you're not out of its way yet," I ventured, glancing around. Sunlight sparkled off her diamonds. Birds sang merrily from the palm trees.

She cracked another grin, and raised her cut crystal glass in a toast. "To life!"

"To life!" I agreed, and we clinked glasses.

"Hey! What's all this racket about?" Her husband padded out of the bungalow, surprising us both. Had the time gone so quickly? He rounded the corner, resplendent in baggy Hawaiian print shorts splashed with seashells and rainbows.

"Why, sugar!" she giggled. "Wherever did you get those swimming trunks?"

"Todd sent them over as a gag," he replied, lowering his head and feigning hurt. "Why? Don't you like them?"

They both burst out laughing. "Get your fat ass over here," she patted the water beside her. "David, honey, will you bring Peter a glass?"

I was already headed for the bar. Before he'd eased into the hot tub, I'd poured and set the silver tray on the flagstone nearest his right hand.

"What were you two toasting?" he asked.

"Life," she winked at me. "That, and money and love and sex! David asked me about my secret recipe for money, and I was just starting to tell him. Guess we got carried away..."

"I'll say," he smiled. "But that's an interesting question; don't meet many people asking questions like that. So what did you tell him?"

"Why, sugar, you know where money comes from." She took his hand and placed it on her chest. "My lovin' is your lucky little charm." She turned to me and said, "I'm his good-luck baby. Every time we make love, he makes another million dollars."

Turning back to him, she whispered, "Ain't that so, baby?"

He blushed and stammered. "Why, Kim, you're being so ... so straightforward!"

"Oh, come on, Peter. David here is perfectly harmless. Don't you want to let him in on the secret?" She nuzzled the side of his neck.

"Well," he admitted, "it is refreshing to have someone who actually cares enough to ask. I get so bored with these pompous asses who think they know everything."

"Which pompous asses are those, sugar?" she asked.

"Oh, those friends of Todd's I played golf with this morning. They're so damn full of themselves. They believe they've got the angles all scoped out, you know, but they never bother to think for themselves. What crap! They're just milking the same tired formulas their parents passed down to them. You know, one of them actually bragged about using the same accounting firm as his great-grandfather. Same lawyers, same stocks and bonds, same everything. Incredible!" He shook his head.

"Forget about them," she advised, wiggling her foot between his legs. "Life's too short to worry about the dead. Even the frigging rich ones!"

"They may have money," he said, getting into the spirit, "but they don't have FUN!" He grabbed a glass of Dom and dumped it out over their heads. She squealed and dunked him. Moments later, breathless, with freshly filled glasses, they toasted again. "To FUN!" I discreetly edged away, deciding privacy was in order.

"WHERE ARE YOU SNEAKING OFF TO?" he bellowed. She snuggled into his arms as he called me back. "We're about to tell you the meaning of life! Now you get over here, pour you some bubbly, and sit."

I did as I was told. He took a deep breath, settled back, and began.

"In the beginning, a million years before I met Kim, I worked like the dickens. Had my own small business, a beer and pizza joint in Wisconsin. The hours were long, but I enjoyed myself, and the money was good.

"Then Kim came into the store one day, and it was love at first sight."

"It sure was, baby," she agreed, nibbling on his ear.

"Cut that out, honey. I'm trying to tell this boy the meaning of life."

"So am I, baby, so am I," she whispered, smoothing back his hair. "You know that actions speak louder than words..."

"I think he gets the point, Kim."

"Okay," she looked up at me. I was leaning back into the shade of the hibiscus, feeling slightly ill at ease. She seemed to sense my discomfort, for she said, "David, honey, let me tell you something: don't ever be ashamed of love. It makes the world go round, it makes the sun rise every morning. I don't understand why people don't get that. Making love is the secret of making life; isn't that perfectly obvious?

"When I make love, everything inside me opens up. That's how it's meant to be. The world responds, and everything inside it opens too. That's how I make money, and that's how Peter does too. Don't let him tell you any different. He knows it's true."

Peter softened visibly. "We don't usually talk about it this way because most people just don't understand. Hell, most of them don't even approve. But let me tell you, it's the truth. Kim here showed me the meaning of life, and it's been easy sailing ever since.

"Within a year of meeting her, I had two stores. Then three. Now I have a franchise, and it runs itself. I wouldn't have to work another day in my life if I didn't want to.

"I'd like to say that it was all my doing, but it wasn't. Oh, I'd have been successful without Kim, but I'd have been working my butt off, too. She showed me that loving makes working irrelevant, just absolutely irrelevant."

"Loving is the key," she said softly. "Of course, sex is the lock on the door, ain't it, Peter?"

He opened his mouth and creaked like a huge wooden door on rusty hinges. She howled with laughter.

"GET IT?" they both said in unison. I cracked up. Did they rehearse this stuff?

"So what you're telling me," I replied, "is that love and sex and having fun will make you more money than working your butt off."

"That's right," he said. "I didn't get it for a long long time. Doesn't make much sense, does it? And yet, if you think about it, it makes loads of sense. When you're working all the time, you can't think straight. Your nose is buried in a thousand details and demands. You only see what's right in front of you. And let me tell you, opportunity is not usually that close. At least, not the big opportunities. You gotta lift up your head to see the big ones."

"I follow that. But what does that have to do with love or sex?"

"Sex shakes you up; it shakes you out of your routine. When you're working all the time, you get caught up in routines: you think the same, see things the same way. I swear to God, I think your body even tightens up in the same places. I always used to get these tension headaches in the back of my neck, you know. They stopped when Kim moved in.

"Sex can be very creative," he glanced over at his wife, "that is, if you're doing it right. Kim showed me how to do it right. Before her, it was just another part of my routine. Never shook me up at all. But now..." He exhaled and seemed to drift away.

"What Peter means," she continued for him, "is that sex can free you up. Body, mind, and soul. If you're loosened up, you can play with life. When you're stuck and tired, all you can do is struggle. I don't believe in struggling. Life is meant to be enjoyed."

I found myself relaxing. Time seemed to slow down, and the air took on a thickness and sweetness I hadn't felt here before. This couple was sharing a very special intimacy with me, and I felt oddly moved.

"I'm honored that you include me in this," I told them.

They held each other closer and smiled up at me. Their faces softened again. We moved another level deeper.

"I must admit I've never thought of love and sex as having anything to do with money. Besides the obvious, that is." I decided to take a risk with them. "When you first told me your secret of money, I thought that's what you meant. Please don't be offended; it's only my ignorance. I've seen so many women come through here who seem to treat their bodies as a tool to get the job done. Some of them have even told me that sex is easier than working, but I thought they meant that it pays more and takes less time. I've never heard anyone explain it like you have."

"Oh, David honey, I understand," Kim reassured me. "No offense taken."

"Thank you. I must admit that when I make love, before I lose the high, I do feel that life is easy, that all the problems in the world amount to nothing."

"That's right," Peter jumped back in. "And what we're talking about is staying in that space, not losing what you call 'the high.'"

"That's where the love comes in," said Kim. "Sex alone can generate that feeling, but it can't keep it going. The rhythms of sex are too up-and-down, come-and-go. But when you add love, then the sex hits you deeper, in your heart. What I mean is that sex can shift you to a different understanding about life, but unless you add love to the sex, the feeling will slip away. God, how do I say this? Help me here, Peter."

"For me, before Kim, sex was only physical," he said. "Now it's emotional too, and the feeling stays with me longer. When I focus on my body, the euphoria comes and goes. When I stay in my heart, it comes and stays. At least, as long as I stay in my heart it's still there. If I stop feeling and start thinking, it goes away too. She's always telling me I think too much."

"You're learning, sweetie; you're doing fine." She stroked his arm gently.

"So emotions make the effect last longer?" I asked.

"Well, that's part of it," Kim answered. "But not all of it. I wish I could explain it better. For me, it's like an endless circle: I have sex, and fall in love, and then I want to make love more, and then I feel more in love than ever. One feeds on the other: body and soul, body and soul."

"You must love each other very deeply."

"Oh, we do, we do," he nodded softly.

"I think it's very wonderful for you," I said, "but I'm not sure how to do this in my own life."

"Are you married?" Kim asked me.

"No."

"Are you in love?"

"Not really."

"Then you have to start with yourself."

"Sounds pretty dreary," I protested.

"Oh, David honey, don't even say that! Love is love no matter who it is or where it goes. Sometimes you have to practice with yourself first. Believe me, it doesn't matter. You can never love too much."

"Does more love mean more money?" I asked hopefully.

"That's generally how it works," she said.

"Well, then, I guess it's worthwhile practicing on myself."

"Don't do it for the money, David. I'm not sure that works. You have to do it because you love life, and want to love it more. It happens very deep inside of me. Sometimes I feel I'm calling out to life with my body, like I want the world to be my lover. The deeper I go, and the more I call out, the better my life gets. I have a man I love, and a wonderful life. I can do anything in the whole wide world!

"The money's not important to me. It's just a lubricant, part of what allows the lovemaking to happen. When the world gets aroused, it lubricates money, as part of its arousal. The money allows us to go deeper and farther. I don't want it for itself. I want it so I can play and open up and love."

Peter and I looked at each other, suddenly bonded by our maleness in the presence of this very female energy. Now we were on the outside of the circle, watching her make love with everything around her: the water, the trees, the sky itself seemed to bend toward her.

"I just know it works," he told me. "And I'm glad that she includes me in the magic."

She smiled at us like a goddess, water dripping off her dyed blond hair, sunlight sparkling off her gaudy diamond rings. "Oh, y'all are too damn much!" she chided. With a whoop, she splashed at us both, and ran off to the pool.

- $ -

ROCKET-FUELED DREAMS

The next day I had questions for my little money goddess. Peter had left for the golf course, and she had a late breakfast alone at the edge of the pool.

"Do you really mean that money comes from nothing more than love and sex?" I asked her after she'd finished her strawberries and cream. By now we'd grown used to just speaking our minds.

"That's right, sweetie," she replied.

"Then why are there so many desperately poor people who are in love? I know paupers who make love all night, and money never comes to them."

"You do have a point there, darling. Maybe I should be more specific. Making love creates pleasure, and THAT'S what brings money."

"I'm afraid that's not much more specific."

"Oh, men!" she rolled her eyes at me. "Why do you need an explanation for EVERYTHING?"

"Because we want to know how it works. Just be patient with me, please." I pouted and acted as dumb as I could.

She cracked a grin and said, "Sit down, Bozo. Let me explain it to you, if you're so all-fired intent on understanding. Now, where do I begin?

"You have to want something first, if you want it to happen. You need to want it a lot, not just a little. Then you have to believe that your dream will come true.

"The love is just an energizer; it gives you umpphh! and power. Emotion is the strongest power in the world, did you know that? And sex is the best way I know of to create emotion."

I interrupted. "So you're just using sex to generate emotion?"

"Not just any emotion, David. *Love*. Any old emotion will get people moving, but love is what brings home the bacon."

"I don't get it. Let's say that sex can create love: that I'll buy. I know that it creates a lot of other emotions, too, but we're not worried about those right now."

"That's right. If you use sex to make jealousy or anger or guilt, then you're not even close to what I'm talking about. You have to use sex to make love."

"OK, fine. So you're using sex to create love. I understand that. I don't always know how to do it, but at least I know what you're talking about. What I don't get is, how do you make money out of love?"

"That's exactly what you do, silly. You make money out of love. Is there anything on earth more valuable than love?"

"Not that I can think of."

"How much money is spent every day to buy love, to attract love, to bring us one little-bitty inch closer to love?"

"The GNP of California, at least. So what's your point?"

"Love creates everything. It's the source of everything we long for, and everything we do. Anyone who knows how to love is absolutely invaluable. Anyone who knows how to love on command is absolutely invincible. No one can resist the power of love."

"You should write songs."

"Someday, when I run out of other things to do, I will." She winked at me.

"But in the meantime..."

"In the meantime, I'm too busy with loving to bother. Besides," she added, waving around, "those birds are doing just fine, and that ocean cracking out there on the reef, and the palm fronds clicking up there in the trees. Plenty of music, Lord knows it doesn't need me writing songs, too."

"Point taken," I conceded. "So now, back to our regularly scheduled program..."

"Oh, don't be such a shit," she scolded. "This is too pretty to be just another sixty-second commercial. Why, if you can appreciate this, then you're one step closer to understanding what I'm telling you about." She glared at me. "What I'm spending my *valuable* time telling you about, when I could be floating in the pool."

"Be my guest," I jumped up and drew back her chair. "I can drag this out of you, wet or dry."

She dove in and splashed about, then hauled herself up onto a pool float. Her face was angelic again, except for the crinkles of mischief in the corners of her eyes.

"Feel better now?" I asked.

"You bet, sugar. I just love the water. Always have. Now then, what was it that you so desperately wanted to know?"

"Well, I understand about love being powerful. I even agree with it. What I don't understand is how love can make money."

"Oh, honey, that's it! Love CAN make money. It doesn't have to, but it can. If all you truly want is a marriage, or a family, or a house, or great friends, then that's all you'll get. Most people don't dream big enough. They don't know you can have it all. They don't even think it's decent to want to have it all.

"Let me see if I can give you an example. I know how you love those examples," she teased. "OK, I got it. Let's say that love is the fuel in a rocket. Build up enough fuel, and you can shoot yourself up to the moon.

"But the fuel's only half of it, darling. You need a rocket to put it into. A rocket with directions and a compass and a steering wheel, or whatever it is that rockets have. You know what I mean," she looked at me hopefully.

"Yes, I do. I get it." I said, letting her off the hook for a moment. "The rocket is your goals, and the love is your fuel. Actually, I'll bet any emotion can be fuel. I've seen people motivated by fear or anger get just as far as anyone motivated by love."

"They may get far, but believe me, sweetie, they won't last. And they certainly won't be happy with the ride."

"Maybe not, but they can be successful. I've seen lots of them coming through here, who chased money and caught it.

You're right about their happiness, though; at least I believe that you're right. They don't seem to enjoy themselves as much as people who do it for love.

"But, anyway, let's not get sidetracked. I'm almost beginning to understand about money and love. If the rocket is guided by your wishes and fantasies -- "

"No!" she stopped me flat. "It's not about wishes and fantasies. Wishes are too wishy-washy, and fantasies are usually second-hand. Your dreams need to be very clear. If you're vague, if you vaguely wish your life was better, it won't happen. You've got to be very specific."

"Goals, you mean. You've got to have goals."

"Sort of. I never sat down and made up a list, if that's what you're talking about. But Peter has."

"I heard somewhere that most millionaires have clearly written goals."

"I believe that. I know exactly what dresses I want; I designed our home; I'm always clear about the time we'll have together; and I plan every day of our vacations. I get very specific. I just let Peter get specific about the businesses. He's in charge there. I help keep him on track, and make lots and lots of love. That's my job."

"You seem to be doing quite well at it."

"I'm the best!" she laughed.

"I hope to catch up to you some day," I admitted.

"You can, honey, you can. Just get yourself some rocket fuel and a rocket driver, and you're all set."

"Thanks for the encouragement," I smiled at her. "And thanks for the pointers. I'll remember you when I get rich."

"You don't GET rich, David. You already ARE rich. Just let yourself go enough, so you can receive the riches life is throwing at you every single minute. Promise me you'll try it, sweetheart. Promise me."

"I promise."

"Good. Now go and grab yourself a bite before Peter comes back from his golfing."

I went and did as I was told. Later that afternoon, as I

was packing up for them to go home, Kim slipped me a gift-wrapped box. In it was a single diamond earring. She told me to keep it as a reminder until I got the hang of making money for myself.

- $ -

MAKING PEACE WITH ANGER

That evening I sat quietly in bed, playing with the diamond Kim had left for me. As I spun it slowly in my fingers, each facet in turn picked up the lamplight and sparkled. Thoughts kept flashing through my mind, memories of Leilani and the psychiatrist, the trucker and kahuna, my grandmother and Bok. Like the facets of the diamond, each in turn reflected something back to me, showing me some hidden facet of myself.

Every time I faced my ignorance, I found the wisdom of a new perspective. Every time I faced my fear, I found healing and strength. I was beginning to like this new game!

Just keep turning the diamond, I thought, and eventually you'll see every facet. After you've seen every facet, then you'll know the diamond itself, its size and shape and color, its angles and reflections, the relationships of all those separate parts. The thought of knowing the entire diamond drove me on, though I was sorely tempted at each turn to stop, and take its partial wisdom for the wisdom of the whole.

Kim's approach to money and sex and love excited me, though I still wasn't sure how to put it into action. Every time I tried to feel sexual about life, my insides knotted up. There was something I was missing.

As I sat there, spinning the diamond earring between my fingers, all these thoughts disjointedly rolled through my head. How do I tie this together? Kim and Leilani have shown me feminine wisdom and action. What would be a more masculine wisdom? How could I tap into something deeper than the trucker's power-hungry greed? JF was learning about service in his new car-cleaning business, and he was attracting more clients. I wanted some way more powerful...

What did I still need to learn about power?

My reverie was interrupted by a phone call from Leilani. She was calling from one of the hotels, and said she had received a message for me. In one of her dreams the night before a shaman had appeared, approaching through a forest and then sitting beside her on a fallen log. He was tall and handsome, she said. The sunlight kept flickering across his face as it fell through the leaves. He said he'd been trying to contact me.

What did he want? I asked her. He had something to teach me about anger; that was all he would say. I thanked her and said good night.

Why was anger coming up again? I wanted to know about power! Ever since the trucker had left, I'd had few occasions to get angry. With Kim, I'd felt just excitement and love. What did anger have to do with any of that?

Because the message came from Leilani, I decided to pay attention. And so I focused that attention back inside myself, back to my emotions.

Just before I fell asleep, I tried to conjure up this mysterious shaman's face. I could picture someone back in the shadows, but I couldn't seem to pull him forward. Who was he and what did he want with me? The leaves were fluttering all around him, excitedly, as though they were trying to talk.

I drifted around the edges of sleep, and the leaves began shimmering too. The deeper into darkness I went, the more they gave off light. Each time my legs jerked or my arm twitched, their radiance increased. Finally, my ears began humming, and I caught the faintest of melodies flickering through the forest around him.

A wind came, and the branches lifted to reveal a Native American medicine man, dressed in furs and supple deerhide. He nodded gravely at me, and stepped forward. The song of the forest intensified. He held out a leather pouch, sewn with claws and bones and feathers, as though he were offering it to me. I asked him what he wanted.

"Your journey isn't finished yet, my friend. You have forgotten all the medicine you'll need to complete it."

"What medicine is that?" I asked.

"This is your forgotten anger." He held up the pouch, and I saw more clearly the bits of bone and talon which encircled it. "This is what you need to bring with you."

"No, no," I murmured, dreamily. "It's love and money that I want, not anger and old fears. Let's throw this away in the river." A river magically appeared beside us, surging forward over rapids. Up ahead I heard the unmistakable roar of water falling over cliffs of stone.

"You've tried that before, little friend. Doesn't it always come back?"

"I don't want to be angry!" I insisted. "I want to be happy and peaceful..."

"How can you be at peace when part of you is drowning in the river? This anger is your power. Without it you will not reach your destination."

I shook my head in disbelief.

"I have come to give this back to you," he said firmly. "I cannot keep it, for it is not mine. You do with it what you will, but I urge you to make peace before you throw it away in the river again."

"How can I make peace with anger?"

"You must begin with your betrayal," he replied.

I tried to protest. My mouth moved, in slow motion, but no sounds came out.

He pushed me down onto a rock beside the river, and handed me a pen. The trees began to shower us with leaves, yellow and orange and rust, large and round and flat enough to write on. I picked some up, and this is what I wrote:

I have been betrayed.

"No, no," he insisted. "You have betrayed yourself."

That cannot be. I didn't know what was happening to me when I was a child.

"Your parents are your eyes and ears and hands when you are young. They are as much a part of your body as you are of theirs. When you deny that fundamental oneness, you betray yourself and the truth of who you are."

But I want to rise above the limitations they endure. I

want to move into more freedom and power and joy.

"Why do you assume that they will not move with you?"

They haven't moved on their own.

"Of course not. They can't. That's why they've created you. Our children are our own arms reaching into the future, into worlds we cannot comprehend or master.

"We master the times we are born into; that is our task. Do not berate or judge your parents or their generation for not doing *your* work. They had their own to do, which you know nothing of. You stand on their shoulders; what they built is so much a part of your experience that you do not recognize it. It is as common and as natural to you as air."

But what about the messes they have made?

"If you focus on what you call messes, you deny yourself your true inheritance. Look at the world they have created for you! They inherited an earthbound society, locked in its old ways, and transformed it into motion and energy which circles the great globe, and reaches out into the heavens themselves.

"We are all one people, just as each family is one. We are moving into unity with Mother Earth and Father Sky, and all their many children. These are the scattered pieces of ourselves, which we have flung away as you would fling away your anger-power. Unless we come together as one, there will be no peace among the nations.

"Your parents laid the groundwork for the union of all peoples. It is your task to complete it. They have laid the grid; now you must energize it. Your childish whining and blame only separate you from the tools you have been given. Reclaim them. Now."

How can I do that?

"Remember and reclaim what you have tossed aside. All your emotions, even your anger and your fear, are parts of the great rainbow bridge, the spectrum of emotions, which stretches from one end of the heavens to the other. You cannot walk across that bridge until you honor all its colors.

"The rainbow bridge is here, present all the time, in every moment. Within you rise the feeling-colors, in every shade and combination. They form a power tool for you in your walk across the sky.

"I can see that your rainbow is complete, but your own stubbornness and denial make many parts of it invisible to you. You are afraid to trust those feelings you deny, and so you keep yourself tiny and powerless. You cannot walk your full walk.

"The anger and hatred and fear are present in you whether you acknowledge them or not. They are gifts to you from your feeling-heart. They help you know the truth about yourself and those you meet along your journey; they point out the way when you are lost.

"Because you deny them, they cannot serve you in the way they were meant to, and so they fester inside you, in the dark. Rather than powers, they become weaknesses."

Why should I accept anger and fear? I thought they only make me weak and irrational...

"Your fear is your protection; it guides you through the maze of life. When you are unfamiliar with its subtle nuances, when you refuse to heed its warnings, then the fear backs up inside of you, screaming constantly, like a caged animal. As a result, you feel it all the time."

But if I indulge my fears, won't they come true?

"If you indulge them, yes. If you call them to yourself like a frightened rabbit, over and over, worrying them, they will come to you. But I am not speaking of obsession; I speak of listening and honoring. Your fear is a gift, which comes up from the spirit in your belly.

"It is the same with anger. You are afraid that if you welcome anger, it will seize control. Your anger comes not to control, but to move. When you have neglected to take action, anger comes to move you through your own inertia.

"Anger is very powerful. It only comes when you have sold yourself short, or given up your rightful power.

"Your body knows what to do. When you let it move according to its wisdom, it will find its way. Oftentimes you block yourself from taking proper action. When that first begins to happen, you will be visited by doubt and fear. If you ignore their messages, that is when you will receive a call from anger. Anger blasts you through the blocks you have created. It pushes away those who would usurp your power, and clears the way for rightful action."

I am afraid that anger will destroy.

"Anger WILL destroy. That is its nature and its purpose. Anger will destroy the roadblocks which you set in your own way, the faults and unawareness and misguided actions which keep you from full exercise of your own power.

"You fear anger because it is impervious to thought. Anger is the energy of the body correcting its own actions. It does not bow down to the mind. When anger arrives, the body has already decided that the mind will not respond to its feeling-messages, and so it takes the matter into its own hands. Negotiation and thought have proven useless in that situation. Anger arrives to blast through cowardice and misperception.

"You fear anger because you still fear your own body. You favor the advice of the mind over that of the body and the heart. You do so at your peril.

"The mind has its advantages, its strengths and its powers. It also has its weaknesses and blind spots. These can be corrected when you balance it with heart and body.

"Anger does not fear, it does not stop to think of consequences. Anger only moves. There is a time to deliberate and consider, and there is a time to act. Anger reminds you that it's time for action.

"If you honor your anger, you will restore the full spectrum of emotion to your body. This is a great power. You will be able then to stride across the sky, from one end to the other, on the rainbow bridge.

"If you deny your anger, its power will shatter your body and mind. It will destroy you.

"Do not think that you can walk your walk without the gifts of anger and fear. That is impossible. You need the full range of your feelings, just as you need full freedom for your thoughts.

"If you honor all your feelings, without judgment, then

Great Spirit's voice will vibrate through your body and make music.

"To walk the rainbow bridge, to trace the full course of your journey, you must open every sense. You must honor every thought, every feeling, every gift which comes to you. Then you will find peace and power. You will find they spring from the same single source.

"That is what I have to share with you. I have come to return to you your anger." He held out the pouch with the talons and bones, dropped it in my lap, and disappeared. The leaves of the dream forest shimmered in his wake.

- $ -

PUMPING UP THE POWER

My next guests scheduled out every hour of their stay during the limo ride from the airport to the Bungalows. He was the CEO of a major New York brokerage firm, with a convention to lead and plenty of work to get done. His wife of thirty years had come along with him, and they hoped to squeeze in a few sight-seeing adventures between meetings. They played off one another like a well-oiled machine: he planned the business life, she planned the social gatherings and private time.

Though that division of labor was common among successful older couples, it was always a delight to see two pros at work, dancing up a storm like Fred and Ginger. Neither one of them appeared much over forty years of age; both loved athletics. They wanted to jet-ski and hang-glide and go deep-sea fishing off the Kona coast. I didn't get the feeling they'd be hanging around the bungalow much, aside from hosting the obligatory cocktail parties and a formal dinner.

We mapped out the itinerary, with me in the front seat scribbling notes while they chugged Evian in the back seat and barked out requests. Luckily we'd already wired the bungalow with fax machines, modems, and extra phone lines. I called ahead to make a few more arrangements before arrival. These two were not going to stop.

Yes, they had energy to burn. The only way I could fit into their whirlwind was to step back and play a supporting role. By the second day, I noticed that everyone around them did the same. I wondered how their children found ways to fit in.

To my surprise, I was invited to join the Mr. and Mrs. for their deep-sea fishing trip on Wednesday afternoon. They were bringing along two other couples, and wondered if I might be willing to help out; it was understood that they would make it worth my while. I had never gone marlin fishing, and so I agreed to give it a try.

Out on the water, the blur of activity finally slowed a wee bit. The boat rocked gently from side to side as we trawled south from Kona toward Kealakekua Bay. Halfway there, the captain turned and pushed us out to open sea. As the land faded into the distance, marked only by the spot on the horizon where the clouds still hung, we entered the vast world of water. The fishers began to unpack their gear. Men moved toward one side of the boat, and the women drifted toward the other. The only sounds were muffled instructions and the chugging of the engines.

Out in the silvery void, I finally caught a glimpse into the inner world of my on-the-go guests. Even in the midst of all this peace, it never stopped churning.

For them, life was sport. It was a contest to be won at any cost, and vigorously enjoyed along the way.

Mr. Stevens never yielded his position as the star player on the team. He was a giant man, at least six foot two, and his size alone commanded respect. When he wasn't ruthlessly aggressive, he often seemed on the verge of a prank or a practical joke. There was a boyishness about his face, and in the gangly teen-aged way he sprawled his body over chairs. Though he seemed comfortable in his own skin, he lacked the dignity of age and his position.

In the corporate arena, his authority was absolute, and never questioned. His subordinates scored points off each other, but never off of him, or at his expense. I wondered if he ever felt lonely. Maybe that was why his wife and he were so tight.

Mrs. Stevens was a no-nonsense woman, very straightforward, strong and even-tempered. No one would ever call her lovely, or schooled in the feminine graces. She had a handsome face, and eyes full of fire. She and her husband seemed to be partners more than lovers, like a sister and brother who'd grown up together and knew each other's every nuance. Their mutual passion was for what they were doing, not for each other. Success was their common mistress.

They'd brought me along on the fishing trip because they didn't want to mess with hosting duties and food, and the couples they'd invited weren't close enough to be informal family friends. No one was going to hop up to grab another Coke, or pass out lunch to the fishermen manning their lines. Protocol was still in force.

The conversation split down party lines: the women talked families and homes, while the men talked business. All three women were more interested in the business end of things. They strained to hear what their husbands were saying, while pretending to keep up the wife-talk with the other ladies. The power always shifted, like magnetic lines of force, back to the men.

"We should cream the suckers," Mr. Stevens was saying to the younger man at his side. "Show them no mercy. I've been watching Dalton for a good twelve years now. He'll sneak up behind you and go for the throat. We've got to cut him off and neutralize him. Shit, he's got the ear of that whole damn board."

The young turk picked up the theme and embroidered. "I was telling Gene last week to keep a close eye on their board. They'll turn if they catch wind of this deal."

"Damn right. We've got to outflank them. What kind of numbers do you have on them right now?"

The younger man muttered a string of words and numbers which made no sense at all to me. I watched the women strain to take it in.

"Good, damn good. Run them by accounting in the morning. If we can prop up the price for another two weeks, we should have everybody baffled. Throw them off the scent: that's the only way to handle these boys."

The young man nodded intently. The air between them was electric. Both of them were itching to move on it already. If I could have offered them a ship-to-shore phone, they would have hoisted me up on their shoulders and patted my back till I was black and blue. Welcome to the club, they'd shout. Then they'd whisper something secret, so I'd know that I was in.

"What about Thompson?" asked the older guy to the right. "He's the brightest boy we've got in Legal."

"Brains aren't everything," the CEO insisted. "He's got to pull his weight on the team. His work's done letter-perfect, but where's the drive? Where's his hunger? When you're down in the trenches, you've got to know that your team will stop at nothing. Survival's at stake."

At that, the women stopped talking completely. Each of them was too embarrassed to begin again, and they all began to fidget with their fishing lines.

The men responded to the shift with silence of their own. Finally Mrs. Stevens suggested a fresh round of drinks, and the chatter started up again. Mr. Stevens called the captain down to explain some esoteric point about the angle of the line against the water, and I returned to the cabin to get out of the sun.

The rest of the trip was filled with similar talk. It was exhausting to try to follow all the names and numbers. Eventually I found myself listening to the waves instead, slapping against the sides of the ship, and the hum of the engines as she trawled across the deep blue sea.

I must have sunk into a kind of daydream. Their voices began to swell again, and this time I listened to the melody instead of the separate words, just like I'd listened to Leilani and the kahuna man speaking in their native tongue. Once again, I found myself responding to a deeper level of the conversation.

I was in a high school locker room, before the game. Any game, any locker room. The boys were swirling around in their separate stages of confidence and doubt. I must have been there, too, for I felt myself shivering. Why did I have to go on? I wasn't good enough; I knew I'd make a fool of myself and disappoint everyone.

The room was charged with fear.

Then the voice of Mr. Stevens cut into my reverie, and I shifted into his experience. From this new perspective, I saw that everyone was feeling the same nervous energy, the same intense emotion. Some of them were translating those jitters into fear, while others were translating them into excitement.

Some of us were putting ourselves down; we used that nervous energy to undermine our confidence, and feed our fear of failure. I was shocked to see that others were taking that same nervous energy and pumping themselves up with it! They thrived on it; they used it to feed their own strength.

How much of my life had I surrendered to fear, fear that wasn't even there? Had I always primed myself for failure? Was it possible to change, to switch channels from defeat to success, to reverse polarities and expectations?

I noticed that my guests were generating challenges in order to pump themselves up. I was taking that same emotional electricity and shorting myself out. Why did I resist those challenges? What was I afraid to feel?

I was not entirely surprised when I got violently seasick. I wasn't sure how to handle all the aggression I felt humming around the boat. So much emotion! And so little love...

Luckily the toilet was only a few yards away. No one even missed me when I slipped inside and vomited my guts out.

Along with the nausea and fear came a stream of memories. I must have seen every missed opportunity in my life, every hesitation, every screw-up. "If you can't stand the heat, stay out of the kitchen," came a voice from the past. I vowed to make it through this trial by fire. Instead of folding up and retreating, like I used to do, I pulled the energy into my body. Great heaving gasps of breath came; I pulled them deeper.

My spiritual training had taught me to let go, to forgive, to surrender. These new teachers from the material plane seemed to counsel the opposite. I heard them out on the deck, hauling in a fish. The shouted instructions were coaching me, too. "Take it in, hold on, pull harder."

I grabbed at my memories, sucked in my breath, called back my power. I pulled them inside. No more letting go, I vowed. This time I'm going to bring it home.

The boat stopped rocking and my vision cleared. My body wasn't shaking, but it sure was humming. I went topside to watch them haul their trophy in.

- $ -

GIVING UP THE TREASURE HUNT

The next few days, I felt my past rising up inside of me, slow and relentless and inevitable. Memories came back, and muddied feelings, like a sewer clogged and overflowing. One night I dreamt I was a fish who had swallowed a line, and had a hook caught in my guts. Someone, somewhere, was pulling on it. For a while, I was the fish being pulled through the ocean; then, somehow, I was the ocean -- or my body was the ocean -- and some fish deep inside of me was being dragged out into open air. I woke up in the dark, gasping for breath.

The alarm was ringing. I got out of bed and stepped into the shower. The streaming water sent me back into my dream.

The line that pulled and pulled at me began in childhood.

No one in my childhood world had earthly power. No one in my family, no one in the neighborhood, no one at church or school had any real freedom or power. We were in the working class. We all worked for somebody else.

When I was a child, that didn't matter. I didn't know there was another way. In time, though, I discovered what I was missing, and renounced my childhood world. I walked away from my father's wisdom and attempted to create my own.

When that brought me no special power in the world, I sought out a substitute father. For a while, that father was God.

For a while.

Eventually I decided that God's power rested largely in God's kingdom, which was not in this world. And so, in my childish adulthood, I searched out a new father. I wanted him to have the qualities of God, but the powers of an earthly king. Like a medieval knight, I sought out a liege lord from the kingdom of money.

That mentor never came. I never caught more than a

glimpse of his face, through a variety of masks, a parade of wealthy patrons. Each new teacher shared a piece of the endless puzzle, but none stayed long enough to adopt this lost and lonely child.

As I rinsed the soap from my eyes, I wondered if this wasn't just another fairy tale. I was forever waiting to be saved from my own ignorance. I didn't know it, but my ignorance would soon be coming to an end.

I got out of the shower, toweled off, and dressed quickly. That morning, I'd agreed to get up early and go on a treasure hunt with two other butlers. Patrick and Jerome and I, known around the compound as the Three Musketeers, were finally scheduled to have a rare day off, together.

A couple months before, Patrick had stumbled upon an ancient, out-of-print book: the memoirs of a nineteenth-century sea captain who'd traveled all around the islands. Sprinkled in among Hawaiian history and legends, Patrick found a detailed description of some hidden burial caves.

Ever the explorer, he had bought some topographic maps and tried to locate the caves, in a canyon on the northwest corner of the island. He thought he'd pieced together the directions, and was ready to try it in the flesh.

Patrick was a hike-and-bike, outdoorsy kind of guy. Jerome and I were his insurance for the trip. Besides the obvious physical and moral support, we also brought some deeper gifts. Jerome was a native Hawaiian, who would know about the objects we would find. I was a spiritual advisor to keep us from disturbing the dead.

None of us intended to be grave robbers. We all agreed that when we found the treasure we would look, and take pictures, but not take anything else.

We set out at the crack of dawn. The skies were light, although the sun had not yet cleared the mountain, when we reached the cove where Patrick had decided we should start.

The canyon began uneventfully, broad and shallow, nearly flat, in the scrubby desert near the ocean. Rolling hills and vegetation hid it well. It's possible that water flowed through it a thousand years ago, but these days it was dry as bone.

On our way in, we talked about work. Patrick and Jerome and I were the best butlers at the Bungalows. We respected one another, and worked well together. When one of us had a dinner or a special event, we'd all pitch in to set it up; we covered one another's butts when things got hectic.

If our guests went out to dinner, or retired early, we would hang out in the Bungalow office till our shift had ended, manning the phones and swapping stories. I told them about my more unusual adventures, with the kahuna and Leilani, and we never tired of telling tales about the guests.

Like any elite group, with access to privileged information, the Bungalow crew was very tight. Most of what we knew could never leave the office, so we let off steam with one another. We zealously guarded our guests' privacy from prying outsiders, but among ourselves, everything that happened in the compound was fair game.

"The Stewarts were drinking like fish again last night," Jerome reported. "I was there until they passed out at twelve-thirty. I hate it when they get all mushy, and invite me to come visit them in London. As if I'd be welcome in their social circles..."

"The Yakimoris were a piece of cake," Patrick gloated. "Dinner out; in bed at nine. I could get used to that pace."

"Thanks for helping me clean up last night," I told Patrick. "After I got the CEOs from Hell packed up and delivered to the airport, I was in no mood to strip the Bungalow and set up for the next guests by myself. Thank God I'm off tonight."

"No problem, buddy. So what's on the agenda for this evening?"

"Nothing yet. After getting up at dawn for this, I'll need a rest. I've got a lot on my mind."

"Yeah, I noticed you were awfully quiet this morning," Jerome said. "What's up?"

"I've been having some weird dreams. I feel like something's gonna change real soon. I'm not sure what, that's all."

"Anything we can help with?" Jerome asked.

"I don't think so, but I'll let you know," I promised.

We walked in silence for a while. Patrick and Jerome chatted occasionally, but for the most part, I was lost in my own thoughts. I was still digging through my past for answers, trying to understand what had hooked me in the guts, what made me a fish instead of a fisherman.

My thoughts were interrupted by the drip of sweat. I wiped my stinging eyes and looked around. About a mile and a half into the hike, the canyon opened up considerably. The walls began to rise a couple hundred feet above us, and the floor, though littered with boulders, was almost a hundred feet wide. Walking was slow, because of the rocks, and hot, because of the sun. I was glad I'd grabbed a hat and canteen before I'd left the house.

As we climbed up toward the Kohala Mountains, the canyon cut deeper. Patrick warned us, from his maps, that we were getting close. He pressed Jerome to tell us what to look for, any special formations or ceremonial signs, but these caves pre-dated any funeral customs that he had experienced.

We rounded a bend, and suddenly the walls rose up another hundred feet, squeezed so tightly you could throw a rope from one side to the other. We started scanning for caves.

The first few holes we sighted were too high to reach. One of them had a suspicious plant growing in front of it, almost covering its mouth entirely. I had a feeling there was something in there, but we would have had to start out from the top of the canyon wall and climb down to it, so we kept on trekking.

There were a few other caves we could climb up to, along rocky ledges, and we checked them out. One of them had animal dung piled up in front of it, and the smell of goats. These caves were disappointingly shallow, scooped out of the cliff when rock had fallen away. None of them was more than ten feet deep.

A few minutes later, we sighted another possibility, about thirty feet above us. A narrow ledge ran at an angle down the cliff, from the cave mouth to a pile of boulders on the canyon floor. We boosted Patrick up so he could reach it. From his vantage point, he said, "I think there's something here, guys."

Jerome and I climbed up to investigate. Edging sideways

along the cliff wall, stepping over piles of goat dung, we made it to the cave. This one was the biggest yet, a good forty feet in circumference. It was cool in there, and we sat down to rest.

Passing the canteens around, we eyed the corners of the cave. A pile of rock had fallen from the ceiling in the back, and I crawled up it. At the top there was a draft. My dad had taken me into a lot of caves when I was a kid; I knew what that draft meant.

"There's more," I said. "Toss me a flashlight."

Sure enough, the rock pile slid down in the back. I clambered around, poking the flashlight into every crevice. Nothing. Then, off to my left, I caught a glimpse of tapa cloth: a thin, brown strip, worn with age, dried against a rock. An animal must have carried it in many years ago. I edged toward it, leaning back against the wall of the cave. Just as I reached the cloth, my foot slipped. I had found a hole. A stream of pebbles slid into the opening as I maneuvered into place.

"What's back there?" Patrick yelled.

"I'll let you know in a minute," I replied. The next thing I said came from inside the hole. I stuck my head and shoulders through, and swung the flashlight beam into another room. "Holy shit," I whistled. "This is it."

Before me was a long, flat room, maybe four or five feet high. I saw several piles of bones, and shredded tapa cloth. Large stones were laid symmetrically around the room, like pillars, but they didn't touch the roof. Perhaps the cave had settled over time, or maybe they were altars.

The air was still and dry. On the floor, the dust was undisturbed. I was trying to tune in to any spirits, when Patrick scrambled down next to me.

"Hey, Jerome, I think we found it!" he shouted. His voice echoed around in the silence.

I slid my whole body down into the room. Patrick stuck his head in above me. From my position on the floor, I saw nothing more than skeletons: no treasure or weapons, nothing carved, no metal, no utensils. Just stone and rotting cloth and bones.

I tried to mask my disappointment. After all the trouble we had gone to, after all of Patrick's wild adventure stories, this burial cave held nothing but the dead. Other generations had already cashed in on the treasures.

Just then, as I was wishing the kahuna man was with us, a presence swept into the room. Before that moment, we had been alone. A cool breeze passed along my neck, and time stood still. Frozen, without moving a muscle, I tried to tell the spirit that we meant no harm. Someone wasn't interested in listening. All at once, my body started shaking.

"Get out of here, Patrick," I hissed through gritted teeth. He scrambled up the rock pile, with me right behind him. I felt the earth begin to tremble, like the start of a quake. Dust and sand streamed from the ceiling.

Jerome bolted before he even knew what we'd discovered. He had woven an offering of ti leaves and stones for the guardian of the cave, and left it at the entrance. We were down that ledge before the ground stopped shaking. On the canyon floor, boots caked with goat dung, we paused to catch our breaths.

"Did either of you feel that sudden cold breeze?" I panted. My veins were on fire, laced with adrenaline.

Jerome nodded solemnly. Patrick still shivered.

"And the earthquake?"

"Shit yes," Patrick came to. "You better believe I did. Yee-hah!"

Jerome glanced sideways at the cave, and motioned us to keep on moving. We'd been warned in no uncertain terms to stay away. Forget the buried treasure, and the ancient maps: the past held only ghosts and bones.

I would leave the ghosts alone, then: the ghosts in that cave, the ghosts from my childhood, the ghosts which haunted me every day in the Bungalows. I'd stop looking to the past for answers.

As we padded back down the canyon, disappointed and exhilarated, I vowed to stop wasting time on these fantasies.

I didn't need to rob the dead. I'd create life and treasure of my own.

- $ -

BIG DADDY DOESN'T WORK HERE ANY MORE

My next guest helped me lay to rest my remaining child-hood fantasies. No, that's too kind: in one drunken tirade, he nailed the coffin shut, and jump-kicked it into the ground.

I'd been telling him how I'd longed for a father figure, a mentor to show me the ropes. He nearly choked for laughing in my face. "Don't be ridiculous," he insisted. "Those days are over. The business world has changed forever. What you're wait-ing for will shortly be extinct.

"It's no longer one big happy family, with daddy at the helm. When I was young, loyalty might get you somewhere in a company, but now, it just invites abuse. The loyal people get assigned the dirty work. I should know."

By some mysterious coincidence, all five Bungalows were filled with head men from Detroit and Tokyo, representing the top auto-makers in the world. The hush-hush meetings and late-night parties roved around the compound, from one villa to the next. The fate of an industry was being decided here; almost as an afterthought, so were the fates of millions of employees.

My informant had come home slightly inebriated, and not quite ready to retire. I had the bungalow prepared for bedtime, with the lights dimmed and the sheets turned down. He asked me for a nightcap. As I poured him a Courvoisier, he commended my good work, then started to lament the good old days.

"It used to be a gentleman's game," he drawled. "We kept the fighting on the battlefield, away from the women and children. Now, no one's safe. The secretaries, kids and pensioners are as likely to get shot as any of us soldiers.

"When our 'friends' here forced Detroit into a panic a generation ago, we sacrificed job security and company loyalty to keep from going bankrupt. You just can't compete in a global market when you're burdened with dead weight. And, sad to say, if you are not producing profit, you're dead weight, I don't care who you are. In a crisis, everyone's expendable. If you don't lighten up the lifeboats, everyone will drown.

"Used to be, you started with a company, and they would see you through into retirement. Now, it's every man for himself. We're all mercenaries, hired guns. Only the strongest and brightest survive." He ran a nervous hand through his thick white hair.

"I thought Japan was famous for its lifelong corporate employees," I interrupted. I didn't like the depressing direction this was taking. "I thought American corporations were trying to follow the Japanese model."

He snorted in comic disgust. So many different emotions flickered across his face, it was hard to tell what he was really feeling. "Don't bet on it. Japan will soon be following us.

"Now our number-crunchers have discovered the advantages of the expendable employee. Part-time workers, temp employees, non-union wage scales, lighter benefits: this is the wave of the future, my friend. It's cheap, it's mobile. No dead weight.

"The war with labor has hit management, too. When you have been around too long, outlived your profitability, you're axed. If they can't fire you outright, they've other ways to coax or bully you right out the door.

"Once you're gone, your workload's dumped on onto the up-and-coming workaholics, the youngsters trying to prove themselves, who'll work eighty-hour weeks on a forty-hour salary. Or else they pick up someone new at half your going rate. Who can argue with the mathematics?

"Next will come the contract worker, the independent freelancer. The hired hit man. With them, you know exactly what you're getting. Hell, even CEO's are interchangeable!" He laughed a hearty laugh, and started choking. I grabbed a glass of water and a linen napkin.

"Thank you, sonny," he said when he'd recovered. "That's the kind of kindness you can't buy. You won't get that when you're jerking people around. That's what doesn't show up on the graphs and profit tables."

He almost started crying. I patted his back, and led him to a chair.

"We're all on our own, son. Alone, and expendable. Big Daddy has retired. We're working for ourselves; we're solo now. The companies are way too big, the world's too competitive, no one knows what family is any more. We're a rootless society, moving from one job to the next, from one city to another. We've lost our heart.

"And now we have to play the numbers game, like it or not. No corporation can afford to support a family of people past their prime, or those who are too slow or dull or handicapped. All those people get shaved off, like fat off of a hunk of beef. To be competitive, we need muscle.

"Big Daddy doesn't work here anymore. No one can afford to take care of us, to raise us from cradle to grave. No one's training good workers, or listening to the wisdom of the elders. First the corporations caved in, and now the government. We're all so isolated... running away from each other..."

I put my hand on his shoulder, partly to steady myself. I felt he'd knocked the wind out of me. He shuddered. Perhaps it was a quiet wave of sobs that rippled underneath his tailored suit.

So that's the score, I thought. There's no one looking out for us, no one who cares how we develop, if we succeed. No one has the time to take on someone else's ignorance. We're all free agents, on our own, negotiating for ourselves.

My crutches were being kicked out from under me.

At the burial cave, a few days ago, I was warned to let go of the past.

And now, an agent of Big Daddy was telling me that I would face the future all alone.

- $ -

WHO SAYS WHAT I'M WORTH?

"Don't ever let them tell you what you're worth," Eve
repeated. One eyebrow peeked above her sunglasses as she shot
me a mother-knows-best look, and shook her head. "Believe me,
they'll try. In business, what you don't take for yourself is more
gravy for them."

I was chauffeuring a leading lady of the silver screen
around the island. She'd enjoyed the Bungalows for a week and
a half, but today she wanted to get out. Her traveling companion
seemed much more interested in shuffling through a stack of
scripts and lounging by the pool; so she invited me to show her
around.

"Rent us something fun you've always dreamed about
driving," she'd told me. "Limos are too stuffy for this gorgeous
weather." I picked a lipstick-red Ferrari, half for her, half for me.
She laughed. We'd been getting along famously.

As we cruised around the island, on a combo shopping
spree and taking-in-the-sights tour, Eve decided to enlighten me
about the lessons of power. I'd been sharing my confusion with
her, and I struck a nerve. Women know first-hand what it is to be
screwed with.

"Don't let the bastards shake you up, David. They'll try
to knock you down a notch or two; they'll use every weapon they
have. I've seen grown men sobbing on the floor.

"They'll try to turn you against yourself, to stir up your
insecurity. And at the heart of it, we're all insecure, believe me,
I know character --" she shot me another sideways look, and
lowered her glasses for emphasis. I could almost see the statues
and awards lined up along her mantle. Yep, she knew character.

"If they can paint a less-than-favorable review of where
you're at in your career, they will. To them, it means nothing:

a few hundred thou, half a point. It may leave you devastated, wounded to the core, but to them it's nothing. We're all disposable: only the money is real.

"Early on in my career, I let myself be led around. I let everyone else decide what I was worth. It was too good to be true! I was already making more than I had ever dreamed...

"But soon enough I found out they were making pretty profit off my fear and ignorance. What could I do? I got smart, and dropped the damned fears! They weren't doing me any good.

"I had an agent, bless his heart and rest his soul, who taught me to stand up to them. Usually agents don't do that, you know; they want you pliable and scared, so you're dependent on them when the big bad producers come skulking around. Well, this guy was different. He had one eye on the market place -- oh, he was good -- but he also knew people.

"'If you let the market place decide what you are worth,' he told me, 'then you throw your self-esteem onto a roller-coaster. Get a life!' he said that to me. 'Get a real life!'" she chuckled, remembering.

"And did you?" I asked.

"As much as I could at the time," she replied. "Though now, of course, it's easier. I can take time between projects, for myself. I can do scripts I love, instead of building my career. Or not work at all. I can breathe."

We were running up the hillside to Waimea. The car drove like a dream. Sunlight sparkled off the rocks, and the mountains rose before us. We both gasped at once when we turned a corner and the ocean glittered up and down the coast, like diamonds. We exhaled in unison, and broke into enormous grins. This was going to be fun.

"Do you want to go shopping in Waimea first, or climb up the Kohala hills for a bit of a view?" I asked.

"Let's get some more fresh air and sunshine," she replied. "Is there anything worth buying in Waimea?"

"Only if you're stuck here on this island, and you've nowhere else to shop. Good lord, Eve, you came here from L.A. Don't you have enough stores there already?"

She laughed. "All I really want are trinkets and mementos, gifts, you know: island schlock."

"That we've got. We can run to Kona later. Right now, I want to show you the view above the ranchlands."

The car purred, and I slipped in an Enya CD. With that kind of soundtrack, the whole day turned magic.

"So how did you learn to find your worth outside the marketplace?" I finally asked. She had me intrigued by the idea of creating my own value...

"First you have to decide what's of value to *you*, the kinds of things you love to do, the gifts you want to share. Otherwise, life is just another job. There will always be people who tell us what to do. The only problem is, then we're living for them. They get all their dreams fulfilled, and we get shit. Are you following me?"

"Yes."

"If you don't decide what you want to do with your life, that's when they'll step in. You make your life an empty parking space, and somebody's going to horn in on it. But if you've got your own car in that space, no one will bother you.

"So you have got to get possessive about what you want. Drive it in and park it, damn it! Don't let anybody else tell you what your life should look like."

"I'm starting to do that. I'm learning to create my life. It's getting more solid."

Just before we got into Waimea proper, I took a left. We passed three students riding horses in a field. Eve waved a big howdy-do wave, and all three broke into flustered giggles.

I told her about the business JF had started, detailing cars. Neither one of us knew anything about entrepreneuring; neither one of us knew how to detail cars. JF had taught himself the practical side, and I began to coach him through the creative. We made up flyers, printed business cards, tried out marketing strategies. He handed cards out on the street, to all the nicer cars he saw. Then he got into the realtor network; most of the real estate agents played to a more upscale clientele, and many of them drove expensive cars; all of them needed immaculate vehicles.

The hardest part was dealing with the yo-yo of success and failure. A good week made the world look bright; a bad one, and the whole house of cards collapsed in the dust. Financially, that was difficult, because bills tend to come due on regular schedules. Emotionally, though, it was devastating. We went through cycles of boom and bust, manic and depressive. I had a fairly stable income at the Bungalows, so that helped smooth the rough spots with money. Emotions were another story.

"I know just how you feel," the movie star commiserated. "If I trip and make two duds in a row, my career is in question. When I pull the crowds in, or win an award, I'm on top of the world. What we have in common, you and I, is instability. That's the nature of the game when you leave the office and the factory behind.

"Mike Todd used to say that he'd never been poor, only broke. Being poor is a frame of mind; being broke is a temporary situation. Most of us, I don't care who you are, go through times of being broke. The important thing is not to let that temporary lack of cash become a permanent belief.

"I'm proud that you and your friend are trying to make something of your lives. But don't let my opinion sway you: all that really matters, in the long run, is what you think of yourself."

"And how can you control that?" I asked, sincerely puzzled.

"We're all measuring ourselves against a set of standards. That's human nature. 'How am I doing?' Everybody wants to know. The trick is to select your own set of standards, the ones that matter most to you. Here," she adjusted herself in the seat, turning toward me, her hands getting into the act, "here is where you make it or break it. Take me: in my business, the standards are money and looks. I'm not getting any younger. The audience is. It's inevitable that some new face will come along, and then I'm history.

"But that's only if I measure myself against those artificial standards. Me, I want to look good." She had her hair pulled back, a minimum of makeup on. I could see the pale, tell-tale scars along her ears, where the surgeon had tucked away the wrinkles. "But that's a marketing strategy. It doesn't hit me where I live. Some women absolutely lose it when they age; their whole identity is wrapped up in the way they look. I know that standard is available, and I know that many people in this industry apply it, but I also know that it's not who I am. I don't let them tell me how to judge myself. How I measure myself is deeper than looks.

"It's the same with critics. That's another standard you can use. But me, I've known too many of the little weasels. They're not objective judges of the craft. I'm beginning to believe that only another actor can see what I'm doing; I'm not even sure that the directors can. Directors have too much to do these days; most of them know more about the stunts and the opinion polls than acting. But I'm getting off the subject...

"The critics have their eyes on one thing only: advancing their careers by getting noticed. You can't let them define the standards for you."

"So the trick is not buying into someone else's standards?"

"That's it. If I let you decide what's of value, I give you power over me. I did that too many times; I'm getting too old for those games."

"So if you don't value looks, and you don't value critics, what kind of standards do you use?"

"For a while I used money. That was too big to resist. It's a heady aphrodisiac when someone tells you you're worth millions. But my agent put it into perspective. At first I resisted: he wanted me to invest, buy property, stocks, all kinds of boring paperwork. I wanted money to be glamorous. That was a powerful standard! My second husband brought me back to earth.

"And now, the only standards I still use are love, and my craft. No one else can tell me how I measure on those scales. I know! When I get into character, there's things about myself that I discover, that I never knew were there. Depths and places inside of me that only acting gives me access to. That's what motivates me now. I want to feel and understand. I want to feel and understand EVERYTHING!"

She raised her arms toward the mountain, as if to embrace

it. I felt energy pour back and forth between them. The whole car hummed. I thought she was going to explode with rapture, and shout out praise, but as her arms came in and wrapped around her shoulders, she simply whispered, in a voice so low it might have been a man's: "I love this fucking life..."

I got goosebumps up and down my spine, and almost ran the car off of the road. I saw her eyebrow cock approvingly above the dark Italian sunglasses, as she glanced across the seat at me and smiled.

- $ -

WRITING MY OWN TICKET

"God is in the details, David. Einstein said that." We were finishing our drive around the island, drinking in the sights and sounds, shopping for tacky souvenirs and rayon aloha shirts. Eve cracked open a can of macadamia nuts, and offered me first pick.

"Any actor worth his salt knows it's all in the details. Be specific. Generalities work in the theater, but not the movies. We live life close-up now. In details...

"Exactly what do you enjoy doing? Exactly what is it worth to you? If you were writing your own script for this life, what would be important in the end? Don't fuzz out with generalities. Pin it down. My dear boy" -- she turned to me again -- "you've got to be specific."

Our jaunt around the island ended as we sailed through the Bungalow gates. Eve ran in to show off her new purchases, but stopped at a mirror to comb out her hair. "That damn wind felt great," she smiled at me, "but let's not do 'The Bride of Frankenstein' just yet." Details, details.

The next day they were on their way.

Eve left me with a lot to think about. I didn't have a clue, though, where to put my foot down, how to get the paint onto the canvas. How did this apply to me?

I played with the idea of writing a script for the rest of my life. Who did I want to be? What would I like to do?

My next guests gave me lots of time to think. They were newlyweds from Sweden, and didn't care to be disturbed.

We butlers all had beepers, so whenever I was fairly certain that my guests would not be needing me, I roamed the hotel grounds to pass the time. One afternoon I walked toward the hotel pool, and stopped in at the spa. A simple sign above the desk gave me the clue I had been missing. It was a listing of the services and activities available -- massage, personal training, aerobics class, facials, things like that -- along with their respective rates.

Eureka! That's the format. I can pin myself down: make a list of the activities I value, a sample menu I would like to choose from every day. That part was easy enough.

And then came inspiration: I can not only list them, I can decide what they're worth to me. I can give each one a monetary value, a priority rating.

And, what's more, I can reward myself for doing them. I CAN PAY MYSELF FOR DOING WHAT I WANT. If God is in the details, why shouldn't these activities be as valuable as the activities I was already being paid to do at work?

In my job at the hotel, every service had a value. Someone made those numbers up. What would happen if, instead of following the rate sheets other people made, I made my own?

I realized that this was just an exercise, an imaginary blueprint I would be constructing. But it would be MINE, not someone else's. It would point me toward what I most valued.

In my journals, I had often played with making lists of possibilities. Once I wrote out all the marketable skills I had developed; I often listed places I would like to live; I sometimes lined up occupations which intrigued me.

These lists were little more than pigeon-holes into which I might, with a little grease and effort, squeeze myself. I tried to take a realistic stock of what the world could offer me, and choose the closest fit. I shopped for lifetime possibilities and choices off-the-rack, instead of going to a tailor or designer, and starting up from scratch.

This was the first time I had ever considered reversing that process. I started to imagine a world I might build for myself, instead of just accepting an inherited reality. Enough of what the market valued; what did I value?

That night, when I got home, I grabbed a blank sheet of paper and made a list of all the activities I wanted to reward myself for doing. Then, across from each activity, I wrote down what it should be worth; I gave it a value in dollars and cents.

What I learned by making this list, not surprisingly, was that I valued the things I was doing on my own time, more than I valued the things I was being paid to do at work. On the job, I had perfected skills for which I was handsomely paid. On my own, I lived a different life: one based on new skills I was learning and practicing, risks I was taking, gifts I was sharing, fears I was facing.

I valued most what terrified me most, or was the hardest to accomplish. Someone else might have an awful time trusting their own intuition; for me, it had become an ordinary thing. I valued it as worth five dollars every time I did it.

Asking clearly for what I really wanted, instead of hinting around, or waiting for it to just happen, was worth twenty-five dollars.

Telling a hard truth I'd rather hide, taking a real risk and exposing myself completely, was worth one hundred dollars every time I did it.

To a professional writer, sending out a finished article might mean addressing an envelope and licking a stamp; to me, after all the work of completing a piece, it meant the added work of dealing with my deepest fears around exposure and rejection. Going through that process was worth five hundred dollars.

Notice that I wasn't toying with how the world might value such an action; a magazine might pay me fifty dollars for a piece, but I had earned, on my own private scale, five hundred just for sending it out.

At this point in the process, I wasn't concerned about how I'd get paid, or where the money would come from. I just visualized myself as earning it.

With this list, I began to build a picture for myself, of a life which revolved around me and my deepest values. At first, I focused on the activities. I practiced them at home and at work, every chance I could get. I took more risks, shared more honestly, began to teach as well as learn. I slowly shifted into myself, back to center, onto my own power. More and more, I moved into a world I was creating; less and less did I just cope and react to a world made by others.

At work, I got away with murder. I did what I valued, and no one complained. Other people got caught and reprimanded for the same things I pulled off without notice. Sometimes I'd get rave reviews from guests who'd crucify another butler for the same behavior. The more I believed in myself, and followed what I valued, the less flak I got from the world.

When I was true to myself, no one resisted me. Most people didn't even notice what I was doing.

- $ -

THE LANGUAGE OF AUTHORITY

Because I worked alone in the bungalow with my guests, I never had to deal with managers breathing over my shoulder. I got to experiment in private, to create relationships beyond the normal roles that were usually played there. The boy who cleaned the pool was just the same to me as European royalty. No one was better, or worse, than anyone else.

Eventually, as I claimed more and more of my power, I got a reputation as the butler who could handle anyone. The most difficult and demanding guests were automatically routed to me.

In my old relationship with power, I thought of it as power *over* something. Someone had to win, someone had to lose. This turned every use of power into a snarling confrontation, like two dogs circling one another, ready to fight.

Now I was discovering that there was another kind of power, beyond simple winning or losing. This kind of power I called inner authority. It had nothing to do with the other person, and wasn't dependent on them for validation at all. Yet it seemed almost irresistible.

When I assumed my own authority, I tapped into an inner well of knowing and confidence which was very powerful. There was no sense of confrontation, no smell of anger about it. I had nothing to prove. Let me give you an example.

A Brazilian diplomat stayed with us once. Upon arrival, he expressed dissatisfaction with his Bungalow. He wanted another one, which he said had a better view.

The Bungalow he wanted was already occupied.

"I ordered one right on the ocean water, and I want it now," he insisted.

I was familiar with his file. "Your travel agent booked an ocean view, sir. That's the paperwork we sent, and that's the paperwork we got back, signed, with your deposit."

"I don't care whose fault it was, I want that Bungalow tonight!"

"You can't have it, sir. It is already occupied."

"Then get them out!"

"I can't do that."

"Get me someone who can."

"There's no one in this whole resort who has that authority, sir. Just as no one could remove you from the Bungalow you've rented. It's not a question of money; it's not a matter of force. Despite what may be done elsewhere, in these Bungalows, no one is ever asked to leave."

He stamped his feet and threw a tantrum. I waited for him to finish.

"I'm sorry the arrangements aren't satisfactory. I can move you into any empty quarters you prefer, anywhere else on the island."

He stopped and looked at me.

"But I have to be honest with you, sir. There are no better quarters on the island than these Bungalows. You know that, and I know that. That's why you're here.

"When the Bungalow that you prefer becomes available, I'll move you into it myself. But until then, you have three choices. You can be miserable here, for three thousand five hundred dollars a night; I can make arrangements to get you on the next flight off the island; or you can decide to enjoy yourself, despite this unfortunate turn of events. These are the realities. There's nothing either of us can do about them.

"The choice is yours, sir. Shall I wait while you decide, or would you like to have some time alone?"

He sulked for half an hour, made a half dozen calls, and then let me know he would be staying. Over the next few days, I laid on the Bungalow magic. By the end of the week, when the other Bungalow became available, he didn't want to move because he'd have to 'train another butler'. I accepted his decision as a compliment.

Over time, I learned the language of authority from

listening to experts. I practiced every day, until the words flowed naturally.

The body language was a little harder. I soaked it up unconsciously, from living so closely with my guests. I remembered what Eve had said about details, so I paid attention to every little nuance. I mimicked posture, tone of voice, facial expressions, hand gestures.

That was easy. What I couldn't quite get right was the air of quiet confidence. Many of my older guests were simply radiating authority, like a force field, or a subtle perfume. I asked one what her secret was. She stopped, thought for a moment, and said with great dignity, "I have the right to be here."

And so I practiced taking up space, inhabiting the room my body needed to be comfortable. I stopped apologizing, justifying, overpowering. I imagined that a block of space, extending five feet out in all directions, was mine, and mine alone. I didn't have to fight for it; I simply had to claim it.

I began to act as though I had the simple right to everything I wanted. I stopped blaming outer circumstances for my poverty, and took responsibility back onto myself. I stopped arguing with God, and cultivated inner peace. I accepted every emotion as a message, to remind me to stay centered; my feelings became a kind of inner gyroscope for me, keeping me on course.

I continued practicing the work I valued, the items on my private rate list. Day by day, I shifted my attention off the chores I was supposed to do, and onto those I truly valued. To my surprise, no one objected.

When I loved myself, respected others, and did the things I valued most, I was rewarded. Guests wrote glowing letters praising me to management. They recommended me to friends, who would request me when they came for their own Bungalow experience. And best of all, they tipped extravagantly.

I was being paid to do what I wanted. Every night, I tallied up what I had earned off my rate list. I kept a running score, and every month I counted up the extra money which I had received. Neck in neck, the numbers ran. The magic was working.

- $ -

FALLING IN LOVE WITH LIFE

We moved into the summer season. School was out, and families were the order of the day. My next few guests had children, so I was often down on the floor with them, laughing and playing. What an icebreaker! Parents -- especially moms -- get soft and mushy in the heart when someone loves their children.

I settled into easy intimacy with these families. With couples I tend to be more discreet, to slip into the background. With families, there is no background: it's all just one big, messy circus. We ate at all hours, made trips across the fishponds to the beach, played games, had fifteen activities going at once. In the general chaos, I assumed that I was just another member of the family.

And the families accepted me as just another member, too. One morning I was on the beach with a three-year-old, the son of an Arabian oil mogul. We were building sand castles, and learning English words for things. "Sand," I said, running the fine white powder through my fingers.

He exploded, throwing handfuls of it in the air, jumping up and down. "Goed! Goed!" he insisted. When I corrected him, his sister told me he was saying "gold".

"No, this is *white*, not gold," I said.

"Money! Money! Whee!" he threw another handful overhead.

I stopped in my tracks. He hadn't meant the color gold, but the metal. Coins. Money. "Show me gold," I asked him, holding out my hand.

He filled it carefully with sand.

"Now what?" I asked.

He gleefully slapped all the sand out of my hand, laughed, and motioned me to hold my hands together. He then filled them up again. "Goed," he looked at me quite seriously.

And then he knocked it all out again, exploding with laughter.

Over and over he filled them up, and knocked them empty. After a while, I couldn't help but laugh with him, too. Imagine being taught about endless supply by a three-year-old!

My inner work had once more led me to my heart. My spiritual work slipped out of my head and landed smack dab in my body. All I did was practice being present, here and now, as fully as I could in every moment.

Acknowledging the full range of my feelings brought me out onto the rainbow bridge. People loved me there. No one ever complained when I expressed an honest feeling. In fact, I believe that it made them feel safer in my presence. We weren't playing roles, so they could relax and be themselves.

I started getting offers of employment elsewhere, in private households. I was offered houses of my own to live in, vacations around the world, ski chalets to staff, positions where I'd work only alternate weekends, or for two months out of an entire year.

These offers were tempting, but I wanted to continue my project at the Bungalows. I loved the variety of people I was meeting, and I didn't really want to be tied down to any single place or family. Life was too good as it was.

During that summer, I broke an invisible barrier that I'd always held between myself and the wealthy. I stopped assuming they were different. I stopped assuming we were separate.

I also stopped assuming other separations. I talked about myself more freely. I began to get in touch with my deepest dreams, the dreams so big I'd never dared to let myself admit they really mattered to me.

My spiritual pathway had always pointed me away from earth, away from matter, away from limitation. I'd never let myself love the earth, or let myself want to be here.

I'd always thought that earth was a classroom or a trial, a test from which we graduated when we'd mastered the lessons and released all attachments.

I began to wonder what happened upon graduation. Where

did we go then? What if earth was the reward for graduating from another place, another, lower level of existence? What if all this beauty, this wonderful body, these amazing feelings, these glorious sensations -- what if they were a reward and not a punishment?

What if Earth was not a classroom but a playground?

What if the purpose of life wasn't study or struggle, but profound appreciation and enjoyment?

What if we were wasting God's miraculous creation by always trying to escape from it?

When I got in touch with my deepest dreams and feelings, with the desire to experience pure bliss and oneness, I realized that I'd always assumed that such bliss was impossible on Earth. What if that assumption was another false belief? What if the only way to be one with creation was to enter into it whole-heartedly?

The divisions inside of me were melting away. I wanted to merge with everything and everyone. I refused to believe that separation was necessary.

I was getting closer to the mystical state than I had ever been before. And I was on the path of money! In some way I didn't understand, I was expanding at the same time I was getting grounded. The deeper into Earth I went, the higher into Heaven I could soar.

I was falling in love with life, just like Kim had said. The desire was deep inside me, deep inside my body. As I opened up to it, the world responded back in kind.

One night with Leilani, as we lay in one another's arms, we began to breathe together, spontaneously, in perfect rhythm and harmony. I stayed with her, matching our pace, until I felt our bodies melt away. We became one single breath, one single organism breathing with two lungs. One single body moving with four hands, two mouths, four feet.

I thought: if I breathe this way with everyone, all divisions will fade away to nothingness. I could breathe this way with anyone....

I could breathe together with women, with men, with children, with animals. I could breathe this way with the dolphins! What if I could breathe this way with the sea, the sky, the mountain?

I changed my communication after that. When I wanted to be close to someone, I matched my body pace to theirs. I spoke at the rate they spoke, moved the way they moved, breathed in total harmony with them. We broke through barriers in minutes. Intimacy was within my reach with anyone.

There was nothing to resist anymore, nothing to deny or suppress or push away. There was no need to struggle: there was nothing to reach for or achieve. All that motion had kept me from settling into my true place: right here and now.

I settled into it with a passion.

Suddenly I had a brand new set of assumptions. I believed that I could be present on Earth and enjoy it. I believed that life wanted me, and would support my presence in its midst. I even went so far as to believe that maybe I deserved support and love!

I moved from struggle into joy, from limitation into wholeness. I stopped fighting life, and began to embrace it. What a difference that made!

My goals began to shift. Perfection and riches, even enlightenment: everything shifted away from limitation and toward wholeness. I wasn't willing to live a half-life anymore. I wanted it all!

- $ -

SYNERGY

Wholeness had its price. In no time, going for it all became a giant juggling act. The more I took on, the busier I got. I had way too many balls in motion: money, God, love, sex, friendship, play, work, home, writing...

Unexpectedly, a guest taught me a simple way to juggle all of them at once. Mr. Pahrup was a British insurance executive of Indian birth. I knew little about him, for he rarely spoke.

One evening I was walking him over to the hotel for a business dinner. As we strolled across the scented lawns, he said to me: "You're different from the others. Why are you working here?"

This caught me by surprise, and I blurted out the truth. "To heal my relationship with money."

"I see. And how is that coming along?"

"I'm getting used to being around it, but I still haven't learned to make it myself."

"There is much to be said for comfort when one is courting," he replied.

"Courting?"

"Yes, you are courting money, are you not? Your relationship with money is like any other relationship: you must woo it, seduce it, and then, in time, wed it. If my perception holds true, you are at the courtship stage."

"I never thought of it like that."

"All of our relationships are much the same, my young friend. How we treat our wives reflects on how we treat ourselves, and our jobs, and even God Himself. Wealth is a relationship, like any other. We bring to it whatever lessons we have learned in all the others."

A bell went off in my head. My relationship with money

was a reflection of all my other relationships? Then why did I have more friends than money?

"My other relationships seem to have outstripped my relationship with money, I'm afraid."

"Then perhaps you need to take the lessons you have learned in your successes and apply them to your failures. What we learn in one arena always applies to the others, for all our relationships are at heart the same."

"My relationship to money is the same as my relationship to my lover?"

"Exactly. Some men treat money as a lifeless object, to be manipulated and controlled. You will notice that they feel the same way, underneath all their politeness, about everyone they meet. Some men battle money all their lives; one year, they're victorious, the next they've been conquered. You will notice that they're not at peace with anything.

"Your relationship to money is the same as your relationship to God, and your employer, and your children, and myself. There is only one relationship, and that is of the self to the Self: all the rest of these are merely mirrors. Use them wisely, and you will see far and deeply."

I was stunned. My mind was racing, already making comparisons, seeing how one "success" could be applied to other failures. Before I could make a reply, we were at the entrance to the dining room. I thanked him for his wisdom, introduced him to the *maitre d'*, and bid them both good night.

I'd already vowed to move into unconditional living, with honest relationships, total self-awareness, and unconditional money flow.

For the first time I saw how all of them were related. Always before I'd played them out one or two at a time, neglecting the others, frustrated that I was falling behind in some as I moved ahead in others. For every juggling ball I could pick up, I'd drop another three.

Suddenly I caught a glimpse of them as something more than separate. If each of them could help me balance out the others, then I could learn how to play with them all at once. The lessons of one could be applied to the others. My successes in love could transform my relationship with God, and my spiritual lessons could give me clues for handling money. This was exciting. This was the breakthrough I'd been praying for.

I ran back to the bungalow, closed the shutters, dimmed the lights, and readied the bedroom for night. Every move I made took on extraordinary importance. I wasn't just doing my job, I was generating new ways to love and make money. This wasn't keeping me from taking care of other business; it was helping me complete it. The way I turned down the covers, the music that I chose: every detail gave me clues for improving other details in my life.

Could I be this thorough in the way I said my prayers? Could I touch a lover with the same respect and reverence I gave these linen sheets? Could I allow money to enter my life as completely and as magically as this gentleman's words had just entered my soul?

Some powerful synergy began to work in me that night. Everything hard became easy. I resisted nothing; I embraced every task, every lesson.

During that evening, as I hummed around the bungalow, I became aware for the very first time that everything exists simultaneously, that all the separate dimensions of my life are really always present, overlapping, feeding one another. I moved into profound simplicity and happiness.

For the first time since my grandma died, I felt her presence, moving quietly behind me as I dusted the tables and brushed off the chairs.

I'd found the key. Everything could move in harmony. Nothing would be ever lost again.

- $ -

CHANGING THE RULES OF THE GAME

"The secret to making money is so easy most people pass it right by." My guest, whose name is sewn into everything from jeans to runway dresses, leaned back on the pool float and nearly fell in. White teeth flashed in a perfect tan. His bathing suit sported a competitor's logo.

"Make moneymaking fun, make it a game," he continued, regaining his balance. "Your work should be a challenge and a thrill. Then, it doesn't matter if you work long hours, because you're never really working anyway. Your work is play, it's enjoyable, you can never get enough of it. If a project fails, start another one. When you're playing, nothing is written in stone. You just make it up! If you're a convincing player, everyone else will want a piece of the action, too."

"How do you get other people to play along with you?" I ventured. I'd rolled up my tuxedo pants, taken off my shoes and socks -- at his request -- and was dipping my feet in the pool.

"David, my boy, that's the easiest part of all. Deep down in their black little hearts, almost everyone would rather play than work. Why, look at you! The fact of the matter is, if you're having fun, your enthusiasm is contagious. Everyone wants in."

"I have to admit that the more I kick back and relax here, the more comfortable my guests seem to be. Some of the other butlers are a bit formal; everything must be just-so. There's a stiffness in their service, and their guests seem to hold back while they're around."

"Then we were lucky to get you. If you happen to believe in luck, which I most certainly do not. I believe that you get what you deserve. And if that doesn't work, you kick up a fuss until you get what you want!" He snorted slightly when he laughed. The raft bobbed up and down in the water. "And I believe I want another San Pellegrino. Can you reach the bottle there?"

I grabbed a mineral water from its bed of crushed ice, and debated whether or not the silver tray could reach him in the center of the pool. Nah, I decided. On impulse I tossed him the bottle. He caught it with one hand and promptly fell off the raft.

Luckily, he came up laughing. "You bastard! I can't believe you did that!" One hearty splash and I was soaked. That seemed to even the score.

"It appears you know what I'm talking about already, my wet-duck friend," he continued, as water dripped off my black bow tie and onto my starched shirt. "Making up a game is the fastest way to enroll other players. In the general melee, no one seems to notice that you're calling all the shots. You can't tell me that your Bungalow rule-book condones tossing loaded bottles at a paying guest."

"Well, not exactly..."

"Not even close. Yet you did, and you got away with it. What happened?"

"I suspected that you'd enjoy breaking the rules more than following them."

"Very clever boy."

"Most of my guests seem to live by their own rules, you know what I mean? They bend and stretch convention however they please."

"That's one of the pleasures of wealth."

"Were you like that before you made it big?"

"Yeah, I have to admit that's one of the first things I learned about success. If you make up the game, then you control the board and you set the rules. Everyone else follows along, so they can get in on the game. Now, if you're just a little asshole trying to throw your weight around, it will backfire. But if you're making something genuinely new, that nobody around you quite knows how to do, then people tend to jump on the bandwagon. Nobody wants to miss out on something special."

I wiggled my toes in the water. "How do you know if something is special?" I asked.

"First you feel it yourself, in your heart. It's exciting, a buzz, almost electric. If you can bottle that current, catch it in a sketch or a word or a package of some sort, then you're on your way. The package is important because it's the first impression that counts most when you're shopping it around. Go for the knockout. If you can knock their socks off at the opening bell, the fight is over. It's a lot easier than duking it out, round by round.

"Some of my clothes are very traditional, nothing really innovative or off-the-wall. The buzz is in the packaging.

"You have to do something different, something special. You've got to change the rules of the game, so the odds are balanced in your favor. Be the *most* anything; it doesn't matter what. Set yourself apart from the rest on any scale you choose. Be the biggest, the best, the quickest, the friendliest, the most reliable. Be the hardest or the easiest, the cheapest or the most expensive. Be the most traditional or the most controversial. It doesn't matter what sets you apart, so long as something does."

"So uniqueness is what counts?"

"It's the easiest way to stand out. In the general jumble of the marketplace, you've got to define how you're different. People remember difference. You've got to draw attention to some sort of scale -- and there are an infinite number of scales you can use -- then set yourself at the farthest end of it. Better yet, blast yourself right off the mercury. Draw a line, and then exceed it.

"There are over a quarter of a billion people living in this country, and they all want some way to stand out, to stick out of the crowd. What I sell is identity. 'Clothes make the man.' Even more so the woman. Each one of us has a desire to be somebody. Now that desire may be a concept: I want to be like James Dean, or the First Lady. It may be a longing: I want to be sexy, or loveable, or chic. It may be a certain expectation: I want to be taken seriously, to rise to the top of the corporate ladder. Everybody's got a different desire.

"Some of these desires are conscious, some of them are not. It doesn't matter. They get overlaid with other bits and pieces. Some people want to be thrifty, others want to live well. Some want the latest trendy color, others only buy the classics.

We're all constructing our identities, making up costumes for the roles we want to play.

"I'm not so stupid as to think that the average consumer can really tell the difference between the way I pleat a skirt and the way another designer might do it. The sophisticated shoppers, yes. But that takes an educated eye. I know the difference, and it matters to me, but maybe me and five thousand other connoisseurs are the only ones who will ever notice.

"So I had a choice to make at one point in my career. Continue designing for those who recognize, and can pay for, top quality. Or branch out into mass production.

"For me, it was more fun to branch out. That's when I had to outgrow the limits of couture fashion. Best move I ever made.

"People fascinate me, David. I love to dress them up, to play to their fantasies. I sell them sexiness, and love. I make them feel good about themselves. And I've been richly rewarded. There's a mystique we've created, a certain image, and for the price of a shirt or even some underwear, anyone can buy that for themselves, become a part of it.

"They buy the image, pay a few bucks more than the clothes alone are worth, and I pocket the difference. Not at all unlike what you've done here at these Bungalows."

He winked conspiratorially. "Smoke and mirrors, David," he said, laughing. "It's all smoke and mirrors."

I watched him dive beneath the rippling surface of the pool. The next day he was gone.

- $ -

MONEY'S JUST PAPER AND INK

"Money isn't real, you know." The elderly Chinese gentleman sat straight up in his poolside chair. He pointed off towards Maui, in the west, where Haleakala was outlined by the setting sun.

"Unlike that mountain, money isn't real." He mumbled under his breath, almost sadly, "Nothing, money is nothing..."

This guest was visiting from Hong Kong, where he headed an international banking conglomerate. His son was in charge of the business now, and handled all the daily details of their convention meeting in the hotel. The old man was waiting to be taken off to dinner. He seemed resigned to be an honored showpiece.

Unlike most of my revered Oriental guests, Mr. Chu often broke the social distance between himself and the hired help. Perhaps his age and boredom played a part in this unusual willingness to wax philosophical with me. Perhaps I'd learned enough of the Oriental signals of respect -- always walk a step or two behind, never look directly in the eyes -- to put him at ease. In any case, whenever we were left alone, he would motion me to come closer, and speak as though I were a favored grandson.

"Money's nothing," he continued. "That's why I have more than I can ever use: I know what it's worth. A dollar bill is only three cents' worth of ink and paper. So is a twenty million dollar contract... Paper and ink.

"I remember when, in 1933, your government was forced to print money with no solid backing, to go off the gold standard. American currency went overnight from a symbol to a promise. All of the gold bullion buried in Fort Knox now equals just a fraction of the paper currency in circulation.

"And this is no better than other countries, other economies. We are playing in a giant house of cards. Money is a magic trick, an illusion. I know; I have been a magician, shuffling currencies from all around the globe. It is a fascinating trick we do, but we are no different than the carnival jugglers who play in the streets of Beijing.

"And now I grow weary of such childish games. My death is coming near, and suddenly I find that my powers have limits. The world I worked and played in all my life is an illusion. All that matters now is my body and my health and that mountain over there. I fear that all too soon, we too will be illusions..."

"May you live and die in happiness," I said, sincerely.

"Thank you for that thought. Would that you had the power to turn thought into reality.

"Not everyone knows how to do that, turn thought into reality. When I was balancing billions of dollars, I thought that I had found the way. Now I think that I was only playing with abstractions. This was not apparent to me at first, because everyone I knew lived in the same world. They all accepted the abstractions, accepted what you might call the conventional wisdom. We were young and foolish.

"In the first half of this century, the old order of wealth in the West collapsed, the aristocracy and colonial empires. In Hong Kong we witnessed first-hand what replaced them: our own brashness and courage. We had nothing, and yet we created great fortunes. Before us, it was done with manufacturing and shipping and trade. We didn't even bother moving objects. We made money by manipulating currencies, by playing money against money.

"All of the money was paper. Its value was abstract, negotiable. Markets rose and fell on rumors, hopes and fears. Because the governments had nothing tangible to back up their currencies, values could be bought and sold and created. We learned how to do that. We were the financial kings and wizards of this century."

He sat back and coughed. Even though his posture remained rigid, something in his breathing seemed to collapse. In the gathering darkness, I was able to sneak glimpses of his face.

From time to time he flinched in pain.

"Only now do I repudiate that game, and only because I face my own mortality. My son is in his prime; he will live in that illusory world until his health, too, fails. Then he will find what is real, and what is imaginary. All the power in that world cannot keep me alive. That rock is real; my body is real. Money is imaginary.

"Your economy is based on promises: trillions of dollars in debt, backed by nothing more substantial than your government's promise to repay. In China, I have seen governments crumble and rise, and fall again. One generation's promise is not always honored by the next. We are living in a shaky world today. All of our financial magic is about to be exposed. The next generation may be forced, as we once were, to discover new ways to make money real."

The sky was blazing over Haleakala. That was the year that Pinatubo had erupted in the Philippines, and a thick band of volcanic ash was circling the globe, high in the atmosphere above the tropics. The sunsets, filtered through those fine dust particles, danced for hours from one deep gem tone to another. Mr. Chu, through failing eyes, still loved to sit on the lanai and watch the endlessly kaleidoscopic show.

"You honor me with your great wisdom, sir," I said at last.

He sipped the tea I'd brought to fortify him for the evening, and continued. "My wisdom, as you call it, is worthless to me now. I cannot share it with my sons, who are still enamored with their illusory worlds of power and prestige. They do not care to listen; even though they open their ears to me, they will not open their hearts. They must find out for themselves, and they will...

"Money is only a symbol. It is a piece of paper, a contract, a bond, a promise. By itself, it is worthless, like this pebble on the ground. In some societies, this pebble would have more value than a pile of hundred-dollar bills. Do you understand?"

"Yes, sir. I've heard that some cultures use seashells or

livestock as money."

"Very good, that is right. So in the world today, in what you call the global economy, we use pieces of paper. We empower those pieces of paper. We determine what they are worth."

He paused. I said, "A guest of mine from Europe, a psychiatrist, once told me that to each of us, money means different things: power, status, freedom, control, security, the possibility of being loved, peace. Those meanings are private."

"That may be true. I do not speak of meaning, but of value. Money is worth whatever we negotiate, whatever we can get for our pieces of paper in the marketplace. Through persuasion, or manipulation, or force, we must get the agreement of others before our money has value.

"For those who agree to purchase this money with their own sweat and toil, it is worth a great deal. They have traded their lives for those pieces of paper! These people, the common laborers and shopkeepers, cannot afford to believe that money has no value. And so they become trapped in the machinations of those who play with money on a different level.

"Money had a lesser value for me because I knew what it was worth. I was a magician who could always make more. I learned early to diversify, so I would never be trapped by one system or method.

"Other people made assumptions about money, and followed them by working in a single system, a single industry or business or job. I rose one level above. I wove all those different systems together, played them one against the other. They each made certain assumptions about money and wealth. I simply manipulated their assumptions. It was far easier and more profitable than following any one way.

"The shipper and landowner and manufacturer all believe that their wealth comes from real property, from durable goods, from the tangible world. Nonsense! Everything is worthless unless someone else agrees that it has value. That is the basis of all commerce.

"As a banker, I was steward of all those imaginary values.

My business was keeping score. As our banking group expanded, I encountered many different kinds of people in many different lines of work. That's when I saw that everyone assigns a different value to money. Everyone makes different assumptions about how money works.

"Do you know the Indian fable about the blind men and the elephant? Each of the blind men grabs hold of a different part of the elephant's anatomy: its nose, a leg, its tail, a tusk. Each in turn swears that an elephant is like a snake, a tree trunk, a rope, a curved spear. None of them can see the whole, yet each clings fervently to his own assumption, and argues with the others. Perhaps in the end, the elephant tramples them all.

"So it is with people touching money: they all are blind. Each sees but a portion of the whole. Wealthy, poor; employers, workers; governments, business: each makes different assumptions about money. So do different countries. Now I know that the elderly and the young carry different beliefs, also. But you will not know that until you, too, grow as old as I have.

"There is no single truth about money. No one has the real secret of wealth. Each generation faces new opportunities, and discovers different methods. My father told me that the world never changes; that is the wisdom of my ancestors. Now that I have lived my life, I understand what they mean. The real world endures, this world with my body and this pebble and that mountain in the sky out there.

"But men do not live often in that world. They live in a world of their imaginations, a world of beliefs and made-up values and illusions. The contents of that imaginary world change constantly. In my lifetime, they have changed with each new generation.

"My sons will create their own wealth in their own ways. The world they live in is different from the world I faced. What is constant, I am sad to say, is foolishness, and greed, and fear. But the rules of money, the rules of commerce, grow and change. Just as the sky before us has changed, from one delightful color to the next. What color was that sky? When you choose only one, you miss the subtleties and magic.

"There is no single way to make money. The ways to wealth are as numerous as the waves on this ocean. Take care what you assume, though, for your assumptions about money will imprison you. You will be trapped in a cage from which you can never escape, because you will not even know you are imprisoned. I have seen this time and again.

"The real world, the world my father warned me about, the world in which my dying body sees this sunset, is what matters. Only this is stable and eternal: only the earth, and the sea and the sky.

"Money is created by man. It isn't real. Let that assumption be your key.

"Then you will not trade your life away for pieces of paper. You will not spend it locked behind imaginary prison bars. Accumulate great wealth if you wish; it is no crime. Do not let it trap you, though. Money is nothing, money is nothing..."

As he trailed off, I looked at my watch. It was nearly time for his escort to arrive for the evening. I helped Mr. Chu up and into the foyer as his entourage came through the front door. In a few businesslike moments, they were gone.

- $ -

BLACK LAVA INTO GOLD

"Mauna Lani is a billion-dollar land scam. This is all about real estate, mate." Bok, the Australian pool boy, was offering up his latest conspiracy theory. "I've seen it done before, but never on this scale. These guys are geniuses."

"What are you talking about, Bok?"

"The big picture. What's happening behind the scenes. While we sweat to keep this damned hotel afloat, the real money's happening over there." He waved his broom towards the far end of the golf course, where Mauna Lani Point jutted into the sea. We couldn't hear construction noises from where we stood, but we could see the bulldozers and trucks.

"Those are private homes," I said. "They've got nothing to do with the hotel."

"Exactly. Nothing to do with the hotel. But that land is owned by the same company that built the hotel, and the resort it stands on, and the golf course, and those condos going in back there." He stabbed a finger toward the seventh hole.

"What are you saying?"

"It's all about real estate. They bought a black lava desert, on an underpopulated island with a backward and disorganized bureaucracy. They threw money at the politicians, promised jobs to the locals, came in like heroes. So far, it's standard business exploitation.

"But these guys have an ace up their sleeve, and a long, slow plan to fatten the pot before they play it. They're Japanese, remember. They think about the long term."

"That's pretty racist for an Aussie."

"Not racist, just accurate. You'll see. They build a huge resort, with all the trimmings, and a first-rate hotel with fine restaurants and shops. Suddenly the place has class. The lava

desert's worth a bundle. But it's costing them a bundle, too.
Even with the rates they're charging, they're not covering their
butts yet. But that's OK.

"They're throwing out the bucks to make a good impression. It's all about perception, you know that." He put his hand
on my shoulder, buddy-style, like we were golfing partners, or
insurance salesmen.

"I know that."

"The whole shebang is bait."

"Bait?"

"That's right, mate. They're trawling for the big fish, and
they need something very special to attract them.   Something
world-class and unique. What they're selling is not what they
appear to be selling: it's sleight-of-hand, stock-in-trade magic.
Even the Bungalows aren't what they seem to be."

"What do you mean by that?" I leaned back against a
trellis and squinted my eyes. The noonday sun had hit the pool.

"These Bungalows were the final stroke, the bloody
topping on the cake. They elevate this project into the unique,
one-of-a-kind.   The hotel brings in the well-to-do; but the
Bungalows bring in the millionaires. The billionaires! They spend
their money here, then they go out and spread the word. Soon
everyone with money knows about this place.

"But they don't see it as a lava desert any more. It's got
a gloss of glamour and prestige. It's got amenities. Instead of
rock and sun, they think of fame and money. You've got a
magnet for the richest people on the whiz-bang planet. And some
of them are bound to want a piece of it."

"Do you mean stock for their portfolios?"

"No. Land, pure and simple. Real estate. A lot to call
their own. An investment, a vacation villa, a retirement home.

"Only this time they're not buying lava rock on a backward island with no amenities, for dirt-cheap prices. This time
they're buying first prize, the best of the best. Do you know what
those lots on Mauna Lani Point are going for?"

"No, but I can find out."

"You do that.   But I'll tell you what I've heard: the

biggest lots right on the water go for five to ten million a piece, undeveloped. Building is extra."

I whistled.

And then I went inside to call the real estate office. A familiar voice answered the phone; Liz was one of JF's regular clients. I'd often seen her gold Mercedes being polished in our driveway.

Yes, she confirmed, the undeveloped lots started at six figures, and topped out on the Point at ten million.

"Why?" she asked me breathlessly. "Do you have a guest in the Bungalows who might be interested?"

I told her we were only window shopping.

- $ -

STILL WORKING FOR A LIVING

One evening JF went to Kona for a jazz concert, and there he fell in love with Sue. While Herbie Mann played opalescent jazz, they danced beneath the palm trees, with the ocean sighing just beyond the stage.

Sue lived in New York City, though she was a frequent visitor to the Big Island. Back home, she wrote, and traveled in high literary circles. Through some wildly fortunate investments, she'd been able to retire at a very early age. Lately she'd been spending months at a time on the island.

Through Sue I met a group of artists, and began to long for the creative free time they enjoyed. Sue once confided to me that her days were so full now, she couldn't imagine how she'd ever found the time to work at a real job.

I can't imagine how I ever found the time to work at a real job. That off-the-cuff remark became a mantra for me, a tiny seed of darkness dropped into my sunny ocean paradise. Over and over, at odd times of the day and night, I heard the words play in my head. *I can't imagine how I ever found the time to work at a real job.*

I was peaking at the Bungalows, higher than I'd ever been in my whole life. But I was working for a living, still. Before JF brought Sue into our lives, I hadn't noticed that detail.

I was used to my Bungalow guests having money and freedom; that was easy to accept. But Sue was just an ordinary person, no different than other friends I've known. She wasn't born to money; she didn't chase after it. She simply did what she wanted, and the money'd come along to back her up.

That hit below the belt. I couldn't brush it off, or explain it away. Sue was living unconditionally. Her sudden appearance in my life dawned like an omen, or a message. Unconditional money wasn't somewhere out there in the universe: it had come waltzing right into my home.

This irony was not lost on JF; he also envied Sue her freedom. More and more he wanted to play music. I helped him with the lyrics on some songs that he was writing; I helped him buy a first-rate set of drums he could perform on. He encouraged me to get back to my writing, to expand the simple notes that I was taking every day. While I was learning about money at the Bungalows, he was running his own business by day, and trying out for bands at night.

Shortly after Sue arrived, he got a drumming gig. We went to watch him play one evening with his newfound country-western band. It was hard to decide who was wilder: the drunken cowboys picking fights with the Hell's Angels, or our eclectic band of island wannabees.

At the bar that evening I met Monty, a buddha-bellied ex-New Yorker who'd transplanted himself to the islands. He and Sue had known each other for years. Through some kind of money magic, he had also made a tidy bundle.

His independence, I soon found out, was much more than financial. In the cowboy bar, he laid his purse down on the table, whipped out a pen, and began to sketch the scene. I cringed in the corner. When the band slowed down, he did a fox trot with Sue between the plywood tables. Their energy exploded like a light across the room. Because nobody knew what to make of them, everyone left us alone.

I enjoyed playing with Monty and Sue. They took life lightly, and I liked that. They were always available. And when they went to work, it was on projects of their own, at their own pace and timing.

They didn't let anything get in the way of living life.

Especially not work.

- $ -

TOTAL ECLIPSE OF THE SUN

The sun was going to disappear. For seven minutes, in the early morning sky, the sun was going to disappear behind the moon.

I wasn't ready for the eclipse. I don't know how I could have been. I thought that it was just an astronomical event, a quirk of science, another excuse for a party.

To be sure, the island was booked up for months in advance: every hotel room, every available condo and house had been rented. As the day approached, yachts anchored up and down the coast. Tourists without lodging reservations poured in from the other islands, sleeping on the beaches, camping out at the airport. The Big Island was one of the prime viewing spots on earth, right in the path of totality. Everyone wanted a piece of this once-in-a-lifetime action.

I was prepared for the colossal traffic jams, the extra shifts at work, the empty grocery shelves. What caught me by surprise was how the eclipse registered inside of me. The legendary stories all were true: a dragon did come to eat up the sun. I just didn't know that it would happen in my heart.

On the morning of the eclipse, we had a houseful of friends. I was excited to be part of something planetary. The hillside village where we lived, out on the lava plains, was overrun with TV crews and tour buses. From our roof, we watched the sun rise over Mauna Kea, lighting up the space observatories, with their telescopes all trained on "the event."

They could see the subtle changes as the moon waltzed slowly in front of the sun, nibbling away at its edges. If you used a special lens, and stared directly at the sun, you could see a blurry shadow moving steadily across the solar disc. With naked eyes, we noticed nothing. Half an hour later, nothing. People started shifting, chatting, getting bored. What was all the fuss about?

Then, suddenly, we reached totality. One moment the sun was still blinding; in the next, it disappeared.

A number of things seemed to happen at once.

The sun's corona flared around the edges of the darkened moon, licking into space like candlefire.

Darkness rushed toward us: palpable, visible darkness. An enormous shadow, hundreds of miles wide, came shrieking across the sea, faster than anything had ever moved on earth. My body flinched involuntarily, searching for somewhere to hide. The scale of this was incomprehensible: I was no larger than an atom in a nuclear explosion.

Everyone around me gasped, then held their breath. In mid-song, all the birds went silent. Into that eerie silence, all at once, every dog on the island began howling in unison.

We looked around us, stunned. A gray haze, like twilight, had stolen our shadows. Colors vanished. Flowers closed up all around us. In the middle of the day, the stars came out.

I was awestruck. Time stood still, as we explored this strange new world. Thousands of people stepped into a new perception all together. Our differences vanished. On this cosmic scale, we all were very much alike: a colony of ants caught in the universe's flashlight beam.

The sun came back so quickly that I blinked. While my eyes adjusted to the brightness, the dream vanished. I tried to pull it back, to remember the feelings and sensations, to integrate what had just happened to me. But I didn't have the time. I had to go to work.

On my way out the back door, I stumbled over Sue. She was scribbling feverishly in her notebook. In the corner of the lanai, Monty had set out his watercolors. They weren't interrupting their experience to go make money. They were sticking with it, staying in the moment, letting life sink God-knows-how-deep into their souls. We had witnessed a miracle, all three of us, and they were playing with it, reaping its benefits.

While I was rushing off to work!

A shadow came across my face. I felt the dragon's teeth close in around my heart.

They played, and they were being taken care of. Life supported them. I worked, and missed out on the miracles. On top of that, I had to support myself.

Something was wrong with this picture.

I'd been blissing at the Bungalows; I'd been living in a splendid dream. And at that moment on the steps, I had been awakened. The Bungalows had been eclipsed by something greater.

I wanted a life of my own. All of it, every minute of the day. No more spending time in other people's dreams.

I wanted that time to make my own dreams come true.

- $ -

STANDING UP ON ALL FOUR LEGS

As if to torture me, my next wave of guests were all creators: a European director, a Broadway actor, and then a Hall of Fame recording artist. My envy level rose. I wanted to play with them, professionally, to create records and movies and books, to collaborate. But I was just a butler. They were friendly and encouraging; some even asked to see my work. But I had no work to show them. I was so busy butlering, I never had the energy or time to do my own creative projects.

I needed time to make something tangible, something I could share in the physical world. As long as I spent all my time supporting others, they'd make all the magic, and I'd be nothing but a servant with big dreams.

In the fall, when Steven Spielberg came, I didn't even care. The other butlers all were fighting over who would get to work with him: this was a plum position, the epitome of Bungalow prestige. Steven Spielberg was a personal hero of mine, but the thought of meeting him now, in these circumstances, nearly brought me to tears.

That's when I knew for sure that I was done. My work in Paradise was over; the Bungalow adventure was complete.

After that, the job became routine. I went through the motions, but my heart was somewhere else.

I started writing at nights. Sometimes I took my notebooks down to work, and camped out in an empty bungalow, feet up on a marble coffee table, gathering my thoughts. I stopped roaming the grounds. I cut back on socializing. After work, I came straight home.

JF read what I was writing, the first few chapters of this story, and some other, shorter pieces I was trying out. When I finished an essay called "Why I Meditate", he showed it to Sue.

She liked it so much that she invited me to visit a real meditation master she'd discovered on the south end of the island.

And it was he who put the final puzzle piece in place.

Hidden in the hills down on the south side of the island, just across from the volcano, Monty had stumbled on an ashram. The people in this spiritual community had taken him on, much as one adopts a stray puppy. He and Sue would sometimes rise before dawn to join with them in morning song and meditation, or sit down for a family supper and an evening chat on metaphysics.

During her long visits to the island, Sue had grown to love the peace at the ashram. She had many fascinating conversations with their leader, an Indian they simply called Swami. "You'll love him," was all she would tell me. "He's right up your alley."

The next week, she took JF and me to visit him.

We found the guru back behind his living quarters, at the far end of his private garden. He was ankle-deep in mud, with a small pile of weeds beside him, their roots baking in the sun. All around, the jungle pressed in; giant trees and vines leaned toward the patch of light he'd cleared out for his vegetables and flowers.

When he looked up and saw us, Swami smiled radiantly. He motioned us closer, and Sue introduced me. After carefully bowing, he extended his hand. Sue ooohhed and aahhed over some cucumbers and bougainvillea, and that led to a little tour of the garden. Then he invited us into the house for lemonade.

We removed our sandals at the door, island-style. The coolness inside was refreshing. After a pleasant social conversation, I asked if he would meditate with us. He took us into another room, where we all sat on pillows on the floor.

Twenty minutes later, he began to speak. Sue and JF later insisted that his remarks had been personally aimed at each of them, but I was sure that everything he said applied to me. Apparently he'd touched a common nerve in all of us.

Swami talked about the pillars of the world, the four great modes of human experience. Body, mind, feelings and soul; earth, air, water and fire.

He said that each of us prefers one over the others, and develops our favorite while ignoring the others. With a laugh and a flourish, he said that was like building a table with one leg. Very easy to tip over. Two legs better; three legs almost stable. But here -- he slammed his palm down on the floor -- it takes all four to make a sturdy platform.

And that is the beginning of true peace.

Nothing can be built until all four legs are solidly in place, and balanced. Before that time, whatever we put together in our lives will inevitably fall apart.

While he talked, I thought about the moneymakers I had met at the Bungalows. Each of them had a preferred method for creating riches: some used physical power, some drove themselves emotionally, some manipulated thoughts and information, and some created money intuitively, as though flowing with a larger force than anyone could see.

I had always tried to decide which method was better. Each seemed to bring its own set of rewards and problems. None of them was perfect.

In my own life, I preferred the mind and soul, but I was learning emotions and physical actions, too. Did that mean I was becoming more balanced?

I was intrigued by Swami's suggestion that nothing real could begin to be built until all four legs were balanced. I'd been trying to decide among the four ways, turning them this way and that for years on end, examining their strengths and flaws. What if I'd been missing the obvious: that I needed all of them?

Certainly I saw that many people took just one and made it work -- but weren't they unhappy? These were the people whose successes cost them dearly: workaholics who had lost their families, spiritual masters who couldn't fix a toilet. I didn't want to be like them.

So instead of trying to choose which way works best, perhaps the simple truth is that each of them alone works passably well for a time, but all of them together is the only balanced way to go.

Now how could I relate this to money? I'd been telling JF I was ready to graduate, to write the story of the Bungalows, and then move on. I wanted to pull all my lessons together into one great experiment, one grand design. Each of my financial teachers had given me a clue; now I had to weave them together, into something new and strong, something durable enough to last a lifetime.

This could be it: stop shuffling the pieces, stop trying to decide between them; put them *all* together.

The air in the room grew warmer as we sat. My body shifted into an easier position; I let my feelings flow. As my mind glimpsed new possibilities, I felt my soul expand. Swami looked over at me, attentively, and smiled his approval.

"Breathe in what you need; breathe out what no longer serves you. You can breathe in support on any level: understanding, oxygen, love of the heart, comfort. You can breathe in the strength of community, or money and abundance. You can draw into your self your daily bread, new insights and awarenesses, the very breath of God. All of this and more is there for you, in the moment that you open to it. Breathe it in."

He looked directly into my eyes. "There is no need for you to worry about anything, my friend. When you do what you were born to do, the universe supports your every step. Each of us comes to this life for a particular reason; this is our purpose, our karma. When you do what you have come to do, the pieces fall together, and everything flows for you. Even when it seems not to flow, it is flowing. Breathe into that knowing, and all will be well for you."

The next breath I took in, I started crying, softly.

"You have come into this world to bring a certain dream to life. How can you know which dream you've come to realize? Don't worry; you cannot be fooled: false successes will not satisfy. The soul, in its infinite wisdom, does not compromise.

"You can know your dream by the way your body responds to it, the fluttering of love and fear in your heart when it approaches, the firestorm of sparks in your mind as it draws near. It must be too big for you to do alone, and even too big to be possible. If you can do it too easily, or by yourself, then your dream is too little.

"The purpose of your dream is to enlarge you, to open

your life up to God. When you feel yourself stretching, that is the sign God is entering your life. That is the sign your dream will come true."

When I looked up through my tears, I saw that Sue and JF were crying, too.

As we walked around the grounds before we left, we shared what happened for us in that meditation room. Sue said that she felt her friends in New York City calling; it was time for her to go back home. JF kept repeating that he wanted to support me with my dream. He said he knew, down in his guts, that it was my karma to write this story, and his karma to help make it possible.

My breathing slowed and I got very, very quiet. A bird began to sing right next to me, in a banana tree.

Was this the reason I was born?

Was this the dream I'd come to bring to life?

- $ -

DIVING HEAD-FIRST INTO THE FLOW

JF latched onto my writing with a vengeance. Every day he'd ask me what I'd written up the night before. I showed him everything: journal entries, outlines, scenes and conversations. As this book took shape, he encouraged me to make it bigger than I'd first imagined. Eventually, it grew into *Unconditional Money*, and then he really got excited.

His own life got more troublesome. Sue went back to New York City. His gig with the country-western band exploded. He wanted to pursue his music, but felt the opportunities were limited on the Big Island. It was hard to find a decent teacher, let alone a decent band.

The physical labor of cleaning cars took its toll on him; when he detailed more than two cars a day, he didn't have the energy to practice his drumming. He wanted to take time off from his life to do what he loved. He wanted to support my writing, but the money wasn't there yet. I wanted to write full-time, but the Bungalows were busy, and took most of my attention.

One afternoon Nicole invited us to go out on a picnic. We decided we could use some cheering up; this constant wanting but not getting was frustrating both of us. And besides, Nicole was the best cook on the island.

Sure enough, she brought along a dozen of her little jars, all packed with different homemade delicacies. She also brought a book she had just finished, called *The Dolphin Connection*. Some woman here on the island was learning to communicate with dolphins, and frequently played with them in the wild. She was starting to take groups of tourists out for dolphin encounters in Kealakekua Bay.

I read the book while JF napped in the shade, and Nicole went for her daily swim. When they both returned, I was bubbling with enthusiasm.

This was an adventure too good to miss. We could go swimming with the dolphins! Before he'd even read a word, he agreed to join me the next morning on an expedition to the bay. Nicole couldn't come along any time soon; she was needed, as usual, back at work.

Up before dawn, we sped down the road through the black lava wasteland. After we passed Kona, the land became greener. The hills above were lined with coffee plants and macadamia trees; below, high cliffs slid off into the deep blue sea. We wound down to Kealakekua Bay just as the sun came up over Mauna Kea. The air was clear, as it often is there in the mornings. Later, the clouds would roll in.

On the ride we'd talked about the future. All these contradictions were perplexing. Why was JF itching to get off this magic island? How could some place so gorgeous be losing its charm for us? We both felt called to a next step, away from here, with no clue where it was, or how to get there.

JF parked the truck on the side of the road, and we headed for the water, boogie boards in hand. The dolphins tend to swim out in the deeper water far from shore, where the bay curves out toward the open sea. A surf board or its little cousin, a boogie board, makes a handy resting place out there; it also makes the long commute out to the dolphin waters easier.

We jumped onto the boards and glided past the surf. There were fishermen on shore, but the beach was still deserted. A few devoted swimmers plied the water just beyond the breakers. The air was cool, but with the sun out now, the morning would be heating up quickly.

We paddled out for maybe ten minutes, then stopped to rest. Within seconds, a pair of dolphins appeared to investigate. They scooted up to us, then dove beneath, surfacing on the opposite side. They repeated this procedure twice. I slid off my board and motioned JF to do the same.

More dolphins appeared, and began to swim around us in circles. We were both grinning like idiots. I felt something brush my leg; usually I would have jumped, but to my surprise, I wasn't scared at all. I breathed as slowly as I could, and started humming. JF made clicking noises with his tongue.

The water came alive around us. I lost count of all the fins and tails and smiling dolphin faces. My body seemed lighter and more buoyant; it was hard not to laugh. I stuck my face in the salty ocean water and blew bubbles.

My hands touched dolphin flesh: firm and silky, with a little give, like the pillow for a water bed. JF was floating next to me, one arm draped across his boogie board, grinning stupidly and nodding. Their criss-crossed paths stretched out for twenty yards in all directions. The water sparkled with joy.

I let go of my board entirely, and started diving in and out of the water, hands together, feet together, twisting my body as though I were a fish. Something slid alongside me, and I felt a current pass between us. My skin broke out in goosebumps. I needed to surface for another breath, but I wished that I could stay underwater forever. Something nudged me back up.

JF was still floating next to his board. A motionless dolphin, head above the water, was inches away from his left hand. She held that position for countless seconds, waiting for him to reach out. "Go ahead," I urged in a whisper. "Touch her." He put out his hand, and she slid under it. His eyes grew wide when they made contact.

Ten yards away a mother and her baby watched us playing. The baby turned sideways, one eye pointing at us, and tilted its head out of the water. Under the surface, the ocean echoed with the clicks and whistles of conversation.

I swam over to JF. He was crying. I smiled at him, then dove beneath him, brushing his legs. I wanted to bottle the energy the dolphins were releasing all around us.

For a long time after surfacing, I floated on my back with my eyes closed. I could feel the sun on my eyelids as my body drifted slowly round in circles. I lost track of time. The dolphins moved on, while I absorbed the peace they left behind. Once my hand grazed the line on JF's boogie board, and I held on. Together we floated back toward shore.

Halfway home, in the sleepy little village of Kaanaliu, we

stopped for breakfast at the Aloha Cafe. Alongside the wooden theater is a ramshackle balcony overlooking a cow pasture and beyond it, the sea. JF seemed too spaced out to order, so I sat him down and went inside to get us fresh-baked muffins and some juice. As he ate, he slowly came around.

"That was unbelievable," he finally said.

"It's hard to imagine they'd come that close, isn't it?"

"Right now, I'd believe anything about them. They were incredible!"

"I've seen them up close before, maybe ten yards from shore, but I've never been swimming in the middle of so many. It's kind of overwhelming," I admitted.

"Tell me what that lady -- what's her name? -- Joan Ocean says about them."

"She says that they're highly evolved spiritual beings who have come to help us. That's why they're beginning to interact with people, naturally like this, all over the world."

"I believe it. Did you feel the energy in that water?"

"Yes," I said. "Yes, yes, yes!"

"And that one who stayed by me so I could touch her...."

"She was amazing."

"I've always believed that dolphins are smart; after this morning, I think they may be smarter than people."

"Why do you say that?"

"I want to live like that, David. I want life to be simple. I want to live in an ocean of love. When I'm hungry or thirsty, just open my mouth, like the dolphins. When I need to shit, just let it drop to the floor of the ocean. No problems, no worries. No more working. Play all day from start to finish. Make my music when I please. I want to live like that."

"We're learning, JF."

"You're closer than I am. I want you to finish your book. If you just finish it, we can sell it and we'll both be rich. Listen, I've been thinking about this a lot. Our best chance out of this rut is that book." He looked across the table at me, suddenly intense, eyes focused. "I want to support you to finish this book. How long would it take, if you could stop working?"

"I have no idea, JF. I've never written a book before. Besides, I can't afford to stop working. The debts are all gone, but I still have expenses every day, you know."

"I want to pay them for you. Let's go live somewhere cheap. You take a year off to finish this baby, and then when it sells, you support me for a year to go to music school. How does that sound?"

"It sounds crazy," I said. And then I remembered the dolphins again, the feelings I got when they brushed up against me. When had I felt that way before? Oh yes, when Swami looked at me. What had he said? *When you do what you were born to do, the universe supports your every step.* I looked at JF.

"Please," he said. "I want to do this."

THE CAULDRON OF CREATION

I didn't know I had decided, until the day I saw Leilani. "You're leaving us," she said. Simply, quietly. The aloha of complete acceptance.

A warm flush crept into my heart and spread, down through my guts, until the center of my body, the cavity itself, was light and glowing. So much peace and love I felt from her... I thought I might explode.

"I didn't know it until now," I answered. "Thank you for showing me."

She smiled and pulled me closer. The waves I felt came from the island itself; they only focused in Leilani, as sunlight focuses within the magnifying glass.

"I have a gift to share with you," she said.

I closed my eyes, and she led me outside her little mountain cabin. When I opened them again, I was standing somewhere else. Or trying to stand: the earth was shaking.

A wall of silence hit me, hard. I reeled, and earth pulled me back down. A young boy grinned a few feet away, gently sifting ashes, scattering the fine gray powder to the winds. I blinked at the mountain below us. Steam still billowed from the vents of Pu'u O'o.

"What was that?" I asked in a shaky whisper.

He answered in a thick island accent. "Dat? Oh, dat was mountain singing. Do you knowda tune?"

I listened again. Was it the wind? I felt a rumbling underneath my feet, so deep and low it almost wasn't sound. The goddess Pele sent another thundercloud of steam into the air, and then, with a high-pitched whine and a gargle of voices, the lava began to dance. It bubbled over the lip of the cauldron and slid down to the sea.

I watched transfixed. The color glowed so hot I had to squint. At first I saw only the brilliant orange, flamed at the edges with yellow and gold. After staring for a while, I began to see into the molten core. Here color burned away completely, and the orange was stripped down to its primal essence: a white so hot it hurt. This was the core of creation. The center of the earth glowed like the noonday sun.

The high-pitched sound continued. Underneath the molten gargling of the lava, the mountain itself was humming. The air sang with the tension of matter being squeezed into form. Here, earth was inventing itself, pouring itself out into the endless sea, building solid land from nothing but its own intensity, its liquid essence and its fire.

The boy kept grinning. He rocked on the balls of his feet, from side to side, and finally broke into song. The words escaped me, but the plaintive melody hit home. Somewhere in the middle, I could hear Leilani singing harmony.

Each line built on the one before, repeating and repeating until something dense and solid had been born. Out of thin air he was making a mountain of his own. He sat in its belly, scaled its heights, peopled its slopes with animals and trees. He sang life into being.

The mountain grew into a celebration, rocking with the songs of birds and waterfalls, the tumbling of boulders, the cries of the young. Insects swam through its air, and animals parted its grasses. He sang on and on as the lava bubbled deep inside, and the mountain bulged and grew.

Then the blackness came. The singing went deeper, the animals hushed. Life touched something greater and more powerful. Pele came screaming to the surface, frenzied with birth-pains and fire. Lava gushed out of her. Trees fell; flaming rivers scorched the ground. Out of her anger and pain new worlds were being born.

I found myself standing, dancing, adding my voice to the song. The boy went on, as if in a trance. It was night now, and Pele glowed across the fields and through the sky. I felt her rising into me, heating the soles of my feet, boiling my blood. I felt an eruption inside me, and all the solid walls, the very mountain of my life, fell into blackness, leaving nothing but a dancing core of light and heat.

I wasn't singing any longer. The voice hummed through my body, whining through the wires of my soul. I was electric, alive. The pulsating energy beat through my heart, and that beating created me. I was a song sung by something much greater than David. The fire of the sun was in me; the voice of the mountain sustained me.

I looked across at the boy, and he smiled like a god. The wisdom in his ancient, ten-year-old eyes flashed like lightning, then poured over me like soothing water. In the midst of that rainstorm, I knelt down. My knees sank into the hard rock of the mountain, and I prayed.

Leilani stood beside me all night long. At first light, when dawn broke over the ocean, she put her hand on my shoulder and gently helped me up. Together we walked back across the lava plains toward home.

PART TWO:

EARTH

- $ -

AN INVITATION AND A WARNING

Life on earth, as any human being with a heart can tell you, isn't all a bed of roses. When I left my island paradise and ventured back into the world, I was so excited, I believed that I could fly. I had all the answers! The world would support me!

I raced off that cartoon cliff, legs spinning for what seemed like an eternity -- and then I dropped. No wings unfurled. I didn't even land on roses.

What I landed on was solid ground, and when I hit it, my unsturdy legs began to buckle. All my fabulous experiences at the Bungalows had not prepared me for the shock of ordinary life.

As I skidded to a halt, I had to reconsider everything I'd learned. I had to find a way to integrate the magic into daily life.

That quest became the true heart of this book. The lessons I learned *after* the Bungalows were even more important than the tools that I received from all my wealthy teachers.

My tutors had demonstrated what was possible. By the time I left the island, I had learned completely new ways to relate to wealth and money. I believed I could succeed.

What I missed was practical experience. I still had to learn how to achieve wealth for myself, in my own life, in my own way. I had to learn what worked for me, not in theory, but in practice.

Perhaps you've had a similar experience. We've all gone from the classroom to the real world. We've all discovered subjects that the textbooks and the teachers failed to mention.

The remainder of my journey into unconditional money takes some common detours through some common traps. I fell into most of them myself; I have the mud and scars to prove it. Consider this as practical advice from the field, from a practicing money magician, from a mechanic with grease on his hands.

Roll up your sleeves. Grab a mirror. We're diving into the daily mess of living, the struggles and squabbles, the hopes and the fears. Take notes if you'd like. Take my hand, if you'd rather. Remember that we share a common heart, and a common desire to live life to the fullest.

It's time to do the dirty work, to get past shame and pride and fear. The world cannot support us if we're floating up above it. First we have to land, to plant our feet on the earth, in the messiness of present circumstances.

Once we face our poverty, on every level, we can begin to heal it. Once we heal our poverty, we can expand into an endless flow of unconditional success.

To do that, we must start at the beginning, once again. For me, that means to tell the truth about what happened when I left the Bungalows.

Come along: you are invited into my most secret heart, to practice and to share. Together we will pass the tests and master this, and move on into unconditional abundance.

- $ -

LANDING IN THE REAL WORLD

A bone-chilling gray filled the sky. JF and I had driven the truck down from Seattle, and were dirty and exhausted by the time we crossed the river into Oregon. My old friends greeted us with open arms; Joyce was first in line to put us up till we got settled on our own.

She was making soup when we arrived. I saw her through the kitchen window, framed by rain-slick branches and a halo of steam. While we unpacked and showered, she poured tea.

We'd left the island in November. I didn't have the heart to face another winter season at the Bungalows. JF agreed to pay the bills for both of us, with the condition that we move to somewhere less expensive than Hawaii. He'd been intrigued by stories about the Northwest; the promise of low rents had clinched the deal.

While we ate, Joyce chattered away with news of everyone I knew. I tried to focus on the conversation, but the words just sailed on by. I'm not sure she noticed. JF was charming enough to distract her.

Joyce's litany of names sparked interest, but the stories that came with them didn't: break-ups and lost jobs, schools cutting back, businesses failing. As she talked, I felt the magic which had bubbled up in me these past few years begin to drain away.

After dinner, we all snuggled on the sofa, under mounds of quilts and blankets. In her arms, when all the words had stopped, I once more felt the stirring of a deeper soul connection. These people weren't rich, but they were real, and they sure loved me.

For better or worse, I was back among family. For the next part of my life, this would be home.

*   *   *

Before we left Hawaii, I'd begun to play with visualizations. Cutting pictures out of magazines helped make the images concrete. I glued them into huge collages, "treasure maps" to guide my meditations. Several artists and celebrities I'd thus enshrined had popped up at the Bungalows; so had invitations to windsurf, and to helicopter over the volcano. I don't know how they worked, but those treasure maps were worth their weight in gold.

The last collage I made was dedicated to my upcoming life on the Mainland. I snipped pictures of the city life I'd missed, with movies, parks, parades, sidewalk cafes, a giant bookstore. In one scene a writer sat out on a deck at dawn, with a laptop computer and a dog at his feet, and the treetops spreading out below him, as far as the eye could see.

Six weeks after we arrived in Oregon, JF landed a job in a hotel restaurant. Shortly after that, I found a cottage on a hillside overlooking Portland. Up on Skyline Boulevard, flanked by parkland on both sides, it was close to town and work. A wall of windows looked across a wooden deck, floating like a life raft in a blustery sea of trees.

All I missed now was the dog.

*   *   *

In my cottage, I began to write, more to myself than anyone else. I couldn't concentrate on money or the book I should be writing. The Bungalows felt far away, and I wasn't sure how to retrieve them.

Friends listened to me talk about my island adventures as though I was describing fabled Atlantis, or the castles in a fairy tale. To people caught up in the daily grind, these stories were, at best, entertaining fantasies; at worst, they were irrelevant.

Despite my guilt that I was wasting precious time, I had to work through all the unexpected changes that kept popping up. Instead of writing for the book, I journaled.

After the first rush of welcoming visits, I began to withdraw. When the alarm clock roused JF for work, I would go back to sleep. He moved into the working world, while I stayed on in dreamtime. Our realities began to subtly separate: the harder he worked, the more I pulled away. Somewhere buried inside me were the memories and lessons of Hawaii, and I was determined to bring them back. I went deeper and deeper into myself, fishing for clues, searching for the state of mind where magic still lived.

I was looking for the inner roots of failure and success, for the internal sources of abundance. For days on end I talked to no one. All my stories played out on a field of private dreams.

My teachers were gone; I'd graduated from the safety of the classroom. I pieced together what I could of our old conversations, and then I started talking with myself.

I sat at my desk, before the wall of windows, looking out across the trees. I stared into space, and this is what I wrote:

- $ -

BLISSFUL IGNORANCE

Monday, early morning

I'm floating in a sea of fog. Across the clouds, beyond the river and the city, I can see the peak of Mount Hood, gleaming like a distant crystal pyramid.

Below me, in the forest, I see only shades of gray. Trees drift in and out of sight, as though a million doors keep opening and softly closing. One dimension slips into another, and another, and another. In this land of moss and fern and forest, I don't need to be asleep to dream...

The sharp distinctions I once felt between imagination and reality, between the future and the past, are vanishing.

I'm losing track of time already; if JF wasn't working on a schedule, I'd be lost completely, wouldn't have a clue what day it is. After he sets up his drums in the music studio downtown, I won't see him much at all. In one way, that makes me sad; in another, there's a secret thrill that I'll be all alone...

I came here to write, to build a new life out of nothing but imagination and desire. I'm letting go of all the social structures and the outer roles. I'm here to find out who I am and how I can create the life I want.

Like a scuba diver about to explore a secret ocean site, I'm fussing with the dials and tanks and nozzles, preparing for descent. An inner excitement is mounting, a delicious tension, a sense of possibility, and fear. Will I make it? Is there really buried treasure here?

Soon I will be deep in process, with the inner world blooming all around me like an underwater garden, swaying and unfolding. Soon the only voices that I hear will be my own.

I know that once I reach that ocean floor, my life will never be the same. Can I make it to the treasure before waves and currents carry me away?

* * *

Afternoon

The deeper I go, the more I sink into an endless sea of gratitude and satisfaction. I'm being supported to do what I love. Life is easy and rich.
Why don't people want to share this simplicity with me? I feel like a child in a world of adults. Everybody's busy; no one wants to play. Even JF is crabbing about work. I hear them chattering overhead as I sink deeper and deeper into peace.
The sea of love. The ground of being. I feel that I'm connecting with some deeper level of the world, and of the people in it. I'm not leaving them; their hearts and souls are with me and the dolphins, playing in the sea of love...
Some days now I remind myself of Grandma, when I putz around the house alone. I'm dropping details one by one; I'm even letting go of competence. I overflow the soup bowl, or leave the dish towel in the fridge, and all it brings up is a smile.
This process empties out whole portions of my brain, with all their skills and memories. I want to cultivate that emptiness. I need to be silly, to laugh at myself, drift, roam the hallways of memory. This is my chance to break away from the insanity I've called real life. For too long I've been too much in the world.

* * *

Thursday evening

Slept ten hours yesterday, till noon. Went out to buy groceries, came home, went right back to bed. I spend hours sitting, doing nothing. The peace is getting very deep; it's taking on an almost solid quality: palpable, serene. I care less and less what people think, or want of me. I watch the birds land on the porch, the bubbles in the kitchen sink, the long, slow setting of the sun.

I feel myself catching the rhythms of power, as I sink ever deeper into my center. If I sink deep enough, the world will reorder itself around me, like iron shavings line themselves around the magnet. No one can see the lines of force the magnet generates, yet somehow the metal responds to their pull...

I'm gathering the scattered pieces of my life. I will need all of me to make this journey: mind and body, heart and soul. This time around, I want my table to stand solidly, on all four legs. Everything must be in place.

I love who I am. I love what I am doing.

I am willing to go through whatever this takes...

* * *

At the time I wrote that promise, I thought there was nothing more to do than love myself and watch the money flow. I was so enraptured with the freedom, I felt nothing else. After working for so many years, so many days, so many hours, I was still relaxing into the vacation of a lifetime.

I believed that I could will myself wings, and fly above the harsh realities my poor friends still seemed hypnotised into accepting. What blissful ignorance!

Despite the secrets I had learned, I had not mastered money. I thought I understood the money process, but what I'd seen had always been the end result: a wealthy individual. None of my rich tutors were still struggling through their misconceptions; none of them were healing lifelong poverty; none of them depended on anyone else for financial support.

I wanted to believe that I was on a par with them because I knew their secrets.

The only problem was I didn't know my own.

- $ -

POVERTY BITES BACK

As usual, the message came through someone else. Whenever I am out of touch with something going on inside of me, someone kindly brings it up. Not that I appreciate that while it's happening...

"I miss Hawaii." JF threw himself down on the couch and kicked off his shoes. He'd just returned from another rough night at the restaurant. "This weather sucks. I miss running on the beach after work, or getting up and surfing in the morning. Something physical to clear my head out. Now it's jump in the car, shake off the rain, turn up the heat. I can't stand it."

"What about skiing?" I suggested. "They have roller-blading Monday nights down at the Coliseum. And there's..."

"All that shit costs money, which we haven't got. I'd love to ski, but I don't have the bucks for a lift ticket. I don't even have a decent coat. Eight years in Hawaii tends to cut your wardrobe down to shorts and t-shirts. It was a stretch to spring for these stupid black work shoes. Who has anything left for ski boots? I sure don't."

"Don't look at me. I told you we've gone through the money I'd saved from the Bungalows."

"Yeah, you've told me. Several times."

"Well, I'm still shocked. Five thousand bucks gone already! It hasn't even been two months, and all we've done is move and set this house up. If I'd have known that it would go so fast, I would have stayed another season at the Bungalows. You know, when you're baking on the beaches, soaking up that sunshine, winter seems like some bad dream. I forgot how cold it gets out here."

"Me too. I miss Hawaii. When I was waiting tables in

Honolulu, I had money to burn. Go in at 6:00, slam ass for three hours, walk out rich. Same the next night, and the next. There was an endless flow of tourists... Here, I'll stand around with my thumb up my butt, waiting for business, and then two hours later, the frigging manager will send me home.

"Even when I was struggling on the Big Island, cleaning cars, I felt like I had some control. Go out, and drum up business. Or give up and go play on the beach. All the sports you need, for free. FREE! All I can do here for free is splash in the puddles and catch cold."

I started fidgeting. There's only so much energy I wanted to give to such complaining. I wished JF would just shut up and let me bliss out in the sea of love...

"You know," he continued, "this whole week has been a total flop. It isn't worth the time it takes to drive to work. Doesn't anyone go out at night in this lame town?"

I'd been trained from childhood to be nice when daddy came home from work, to be quiet and supportive. Daddy worked so hard! The noise and laughter had to go outside when he got home. How I resented his exhaustion fouling up our home, like some disease he tracked in on his shoes from the big dirty world.

"What about your drums?" I blurted, fishing for a change of subject.

"There's only so much I can take of squeezing myself into that tiny studio. You've seen it: it's like a dungeon in that warehouse basement. When I'm cold and damp already, it's the last place in the world I want to go."

"Don't you like anything?!" I shouted. "Can't you get another job? Why don't you make some other friends? I can't hold your hand through all of this. You're supposed to be supporting ME. That's not what this feels like. We had a deal, damn it."

"I'm doing the best that I can, fuck you very much."

"Oh, for Christ's sake, JF. It's obvious you need something. And I don't have it to give. I try being patient, I try listening to your complaints. 'Give him time to blow off steam,' I tell myself. But instead of blowing it off, you just build it up bigger. Talking gets us nowhere."

"So why are you talking?"

I stopped and caught my breath. "Because I'm terrified. If you don't get this money back on track, I don't know what will happen. We've got a stack of bills in there that I can't pay --"

"You think that I don't know that?"

"I don't know what you know any more. I just know that I can't write about abundance when the bills aren't being paid, and I can't psych myself into gratitude when you're always complaining. I'm trying to make magic here, and you're not helping."

"That's easy for you to say. All you do all day long is lie around and meditate. I go out into that cold, hard world and try to scrape a living for us both. I'm sorry if it's hard. I'm sorry if it isn't moving fast enough for you. But that world out there is real, unlike the little fantasy you're spinning in your head, and I don't see you shitting gold yet, so one of us has got to go out to the trenches and dig for it."

"I don't see that my way's so much worse than yours. At least when I was plugged into the world, the money flowed. You're not getting much more than a trickle."

"This is not my fault!"

"I'm not saying that it is. Neither of us knew that things would be so tough here. But now that we're here, and this is what we're dealing with, don't you think a change of attitude might help? How can you ever turn this shit around if all you do is bitch about it?"

"So what would you suggest instead?"

"Stop complaining. The more you complain, the more you'll find to complain about. It's a useless drain of energy."

"So how does that solve the problem?"

"I'm not sure anymore. About anything. I'm just scared that when you put your energy into complaining, you defeat yourself. You drain away the power you have left."

"At least when I am bitching, as you put it, something moves inside of me. It's the only time I feel alive."

"You move energy, all right. But you aren't building with it; you're destroying. Yourself. Your self-confidence. Your power. I've seen this all my life: what that kind of anger does is make the big bad world seem totally unbeatable. With every rage, you give the world more power.

"What did Kim say? Emotions are the rocket fuel. They've no direction of their own; they just propel you faster toward wherever you are pointed. You've got to aim yourself at something positive. Right now you're digging your own grave, and the more you complain, the deeper you go."

"Sounds like you're the one who is complaining here."

"Maybe I am. I guess I'll just shut up, then. I'm going to bed. I'll see you in the morning."

"Sleep it off."

"You too."

But I doubted that we would.

*   *   *

Wednesday, 2:30 am

I've got to keep myself from falling down into despair. I've got to rise above these petty problems. Remember, nothing outside me is real...

As I move up and down through layers of consciousness, I see my every attitude reflected in the outer world. When I'm loving, I encounter love. When I'm scared, out come the terrifying shadows. When I'm judgmental, I attract the critics. Each mood seems to have its own rules, games and dramas.

I choose the attitudes and levels I will be on, every moment of the day. Inside each of us there is an elevator of awareness. Each time that we get in, the door can open up on any floor.

On each floor, on each level of awareness, I become a different person, with different goals and tools and feelings. I notice only what will serve me in that game. All the other people on that floor will mirror back what happens when I'm playing with those thoughts and feelings.

When I'm sad, all I remember are the other times that I've been sad, all the losses and the grievings of my life.

When I'm angry, everything I notice seems unjust. The memories of other outrages come flooding back, as though they're wired all together in my brain, ready to blow at a moment's notice.

Despite the days of melancholy, or the endless nights of pain, there will come a summer afternoon, when flowers glow along the walk, and I'm in love, and I will swear that nothing has ever been wrong in my life, the world's been beautiful from the first day of creation, and I am blessed to have a part in it...

So when I'm tired of being miserable and poor, when I'm done playing on the fear floor and I want to go into a different experience, I only have to get onto the elevator, and push a different button. The outside world will still play on, in its mind-boggling, sense-tickling richness. Life will overflow with all the signs and symptoms I desire, all the justification I may want for any mood I may be choosing.

If I don't like what's happening, I don't need to change the world, or anyone in it. I just need to change my own awareness. The power to create my own experience lies within.

* * *

Wednesday, 9:00 am

The doors are closing; the noise from the party recedes. The elevator hums expectantly. Is this what I want? I feel so isolated and alone...

My finger trembles on the elevator button. What will I lose by changing floors? I don't have a source of income any more; the instant that I left the Bungalows, I put myself in JF's hands. How can I go ahead without him now?

Without money, I am helpless, a non-entity. I'm a ghost in the material world.

I want to get myself to a new floor. I want to take charge of my own experience again. But something refuses to register. My power has been disengaged.

My ghostly finger, trembling, cannot push the button in.

*   *   *

Wednesday evening

Now that I am stranded on this floor, behind these elevator doors, the other memories of helplessness are flooding back.

When I was in the second grade, I broke my arm. The weeks dragged by; I couldn't wait until the cast came off and I could swing and jump and play again.

At last the day of deliverance arrived. No more itching! No more restrictions!

The doctor sliced the hated cast away.

No more muscles... No more skin...

My shirtsleeve scratched against the raw and puffy skin like sandpaper. My elbow couldn't seem to conquer gravity. Swinging a bat made me break out in a sweat.

It took a while to build up my strength. Those days dragged by more heavily than when I had been trapped inside the cast. I thought freedom would be strong, and simple...

In this new phase of my life, I've sliced my outer world off like a cast. I've dropped the jobs and tasks and socializing, the stale routines which held my life together.

And once more, freedom has an unexpected price.

Gravity pulls; moods weigh me down. I'm hypersensitive to people, what they say and do, their negativity and heaviness.

Inside, I'm raw and vulnerable. Nothing holds me up, supports me, or protects me. I'm exposed.

- $ -

EMOTIONAL BREAKDOWN

Sunday night

This winter strips me down to the bare bones. There's nothing left to hide behind, no rules or structures, no obligations or responsibilities. The golden cocoon of the Bungalows doesn't protect me anymore. Now it's just me and the world.

My original desire -- to write textbooks with all of the answers -- seems beyond my reach right now. Unconditional money?!! I can't even buy groceries! I can't even take my truck into the shop!

I've never felt this vulnerable before, not ever. As long as I was busy working and surviving, I never had to put my very deepest dreams out on the line. I did what other people told me to do; I followed the script; I played a part. I never risked exposing the real me.

I could sweat ice, and vomit right now. Something very old is stuck in me, and I'm not sure how to get it out. I want to let in new energy and life. Please help me. Please help me.

My outside life is simpler now -- I stay at home, I write, I play -- but I'm not simple inside yet. I'm holding back, convinced that no one understands, trying to do it alone. I'm still at odds with life; the world and I seem to be enemies.

I'm embarrassed. Ashamed. Mad at myself for being so stubborn. Scared to let my power go, scared to slip back into victim hell. But I'm already back in victim hell...

How do I move through this? I ache all over, and I'm freezing cold. I want to take another long hot shower, drain the water tank, feel warm and safe and present once again.

I'm scared. I'm scared I won't be taken care of, now that I'm exposed and vulnerable. Every day it feels the floor is tilting, and the rug is slipping out from under me...

I'm scared I'll break this situation with my fears and doubts. How can I accept this much support? How can I deserve this?

I'm scared that it won't last. This is not the first time that I've tried to soar above the ordinary world. Deep inside me are the scars of all those other crashes...

* * *

I remember when the world was simple, and I was grateful all the time.

When we were babies, in the summers we would go to grandma's house. She'd sit with us on the back porch, and set our playpen in the breeze.

Sometimes, lulled by traffic and the trees, I'd fall asleep and dream. My grandma says that when I was asleep, I'd reach out for the bottle with my chubby little fingers. When I found it, I'd say drowsily, to no one in particular, a simple "T'ank you". Eyes still closed, I'd guide the nipple to my mouth.

Twenty years later, life wasn't so simple. For a few years after college, I worked in state and private psychiatric hospitals, with the retarded and autistic and emotionally disturbed. One day it hit me out of nowhere that the staff had an investment in keeping patients sick. No one ever broke the cycle; even patients who recovered were soon back. They'd been discharged into the same hopeless environments. We weren't giving them the skills and help they needed to break free.

Soon after that I left my job. No matter how I tried, I couldn't find the motivation to return to work. Any work. When I lost my apartment, I camped out on my grandma's floor. All night long I'd sit up writing in my journal, trying to think through my grief, to reason a way out of this impasse.

Grandma wanted to help, but I had broken all the rules she knew, and I was treading unfamiliar waters. "You have to work," she'd say, bewildered. It was a fact of life: you have to breathe; you have to eat; and with exactly the same degree of necessity, you have to work.

But I refused. I fell apart on her dining room floor, for days that stretched on into weeks. I couldn't fathom living a life without joy; I couldn't imagine working at a job just for survival. My willfulness bled into rage and pain and finally numbness. I had a nervous breakdown on that floor, right in front of her.

I sat and stared out the window until I finally got too numb to care. Then I got up and found work in a neighborhood restaurant. At least in that environment, I had no expectations. I learned to go through the motions, like everyone else. Shortly after that, I moved to California.

In California I found people who refused to be numb. They had their nervous breakdowns on the street, and didn't care who watched. Some of them had left behind security, and loved living out on the edge. Everyone I met, secure and insecure alike, had high expectations, for this was California in its golden years, and the future could only get brighter.

Drudgery was simply not an option. People were serious about having fun, and played at stretching the limits of sense. I met people who were into metaphysics, manifesting, affirmations and dreams. They understood that ordinary life and quiet desperation were not the way to go.

My entree to this crowd was a man named, oddly enough, Strange de Jim. In this group his name did not stand out. Strange had fallen in with a merry band of manifesters, and written a delightful little book, entitled *Visioning*, about what happened next. *Visioning* was in the bookstores; I was in San Francisco; one thing led to another; and before I knew what hit me, I was going to a Manifesting Workshop with the people he had written about in his book.

That first brush sent me flying. I was high for weeks, attending classes, writing in my Manifesting Notebook, analyzing my dreams, swapping stories with the other true believers. I got great results -- miraculous results -- when I focused on experiences and relationships. When I tried to manifest jewels, cars and jobs, though, nothing clicked.

There couldn't be anything wrong with the system --

everyone else was making miracles -- so there must be something wrong with me. In our group meetings, I shared my successes and hid my failures. Off on my own, in true workaholic fashion, I tried even harder.

One of my favorite tools was the Manifesting Notebook. I kept mine up every day. On one side of the page I'd write the things I wanted to have happen to me, and on the other side I'd write the things I had received. Acknowledging the good that came to me was relatively easy; even as a baby, I was thanking my fingers for finding the bottle. As I became more conscious of my blessings, there were always more to be thankful for. I liked that part of the process.

Zeroing in on what I wanted to have happen was a different story. When I look back over those notebooks now, I see how mushy and naive I was. The only specifics were ridiculously beyond my acceptance level: a sky-blue Mercedes convertible, a beach house in Carmel. I didn't know myself well enough to know what I really needed; I was recycling, for the most part, other people's fantasies.

We were encouraged in the workshops to find our own dreams and purpose, to connect with intuition and our private inner guidance. I faithfully recorded dreams and fantasies, random inspirations and longer channeled messages. I have notebooks filled with prayers and conversations I had with my higher self, my guides, my angels.

When I asked them about spiritual things, they came through with flying colors. This was territory they knew well. My wisdom deepened, and my understanding of the inner planes increased dramatically.

I'd ask them practical questions, too: about job interviews, people, events to attend or avoid, places to go, timing. Like well-meaning older relatives, they always had advice to give about the outer world; but like well-meaning older relatives, they were sorely out of touch. The world they knew was not the world that I lived in. I'd go where I was guided, do what I was told to do. Things bombed, fell through, or fizzled. My intuition couldn't always help me in the world of matter.

In time, I came to suspect that my inner guides were flawed. Their practical advice never worked. I kept this secret for a while, and then I turned them off completely. Only now do I begin to realize that if you want spiritual wisdom, ask a spirit; and if you want financial wisdom, ask a banker. Each of us has our own area of expertise.

I didn't notice at the time that my approach was so completely passive. I had my palms out, like a panhandler, begging life for miracles every day. Never did I focus on what I wanted to create or give back to life. The power was outside of me; I wasn't yet an equal in the game.

The people in these Manifesting Workshops had discovered an Aladdin's lamp: the powers of the higher mind. We were running on spiritual energy, feeding off dreams and intuitions and inner openings. We were focused exclusively on the power of positive thinking, on affirmations and abundance, mental drive and willpower. Negativity and fear got swept under the rug.

When we met in groups, we generated a remarkable enthusiasm, just like any great sales convention or cheerleading squad. That group energy carried us over many thresholds, but it never hit us where we really lived. It never addressed our weaknesses and fears, the investment we had in old patterns, the attachment we felt to our self-images and pain. When someone brought those issues up, they were dismissively told to forgive more, and the subject was changed back to miracles.

As long as we were feeding off the group energy, we could jump over a lot of those old limitations. But to be members in good standing with the group, we had to be relentlessly upbeat, and back that up with proof. Eventually, someone would hit a personal block the group didn't know how to deal with, and that person would be ostracized, as though their doubts might be contagious.

Without group support to bridge those inner gaps, the shaky new foundations of their self-esteem would crumble, and personal manifesting power would sputter to a halt. We could do magic when the lightning struck, but none of us was wired up to generate it on our own.

In time, I too hit my brick wall. I couldn't find the cash to get me into higher levels of the Manifesting Workshops. The other members of the group continued on without me.

After the high came the crash. I was out of the game, once more banished to the ordinary world. I got an ordinary job, and began to pile up ordinary debts. The gates of paradise clanged shut against me.

In my California Manifesting Days, I was playing with a toy. I was young. One dream was as good as another; we borrowed and traded them like playing cards.

Now I'd whittled all those fantasies away. This wasn't any more about a million bucks, a private jet, a long vacation at the Bungalows. This was about me. Who I was, not what I wanted to consume.

I wasn't out to simply win the lottery; that would be dumb luck, a one-shot fluke, mere chance, nothing personal.

I wanted to *make* money: to create it, from the depths of who I was, from my own skill and love and understanding. I wanted to be able to create abundance over and over, anywhere, anytime.

I craved the kind of confidence and power I'd discovered at the Bungalows. Those millionaires and billionaires had changed my mind and my beliefs about the ways to wealth.

Unfortunately, I still had to change my heart.

* * *

Most of that winter I flailed around, blaming, emoting, feeling sorry for myself. I knew I couldn't think my way out of this one; I'd tried that already at Grandma's. Thinking wasn't powerful enough.

I couldn't fall back on group energy. I had no group supporting me.

Remembering the advice of Kim and my dream shaman, I tried to hold on to my feelings, to reclaim my anger and fear, to pump myself up with emotion. I became a raging mess, spewing anger, sulking, crying all night long. JF, poor soul, got caught up in the hurricane at home, and then, when I'd collapsed, went back out to the world to work.

This went on, I am ashamed to say, for weeks. I didn't realize then there was a difference between honoring what I felt, and indulging in it endlessly. Instead of treating my emotions with respect, as messengers about reality, as valued partners, I used them as fuel for the fire. When the fuel ran low, I poured on gasoline.

And so my feelings blazed. I burned everything inside of me, invented reasons to feel more, and finally exhausted my resources, past and future. No more dreams, and no more memories. With nothing left to burn, the fires sputtered out.

Emotions by themselves would not release me. Emptied beyond hope or fear or caring, I laid down among the cold black ashes, and I slept.

- $ -

RETURN TO CENTER

Thursday afternoon

    This morning, I woke up from a dream: I was wandering through the Kingdom, asking every one, "What day is this?" I'd been asleep for years, my eyes were swollen shut, I couldn't find my way...
    Everyone I talked to in my dream said the same thing: "It is the first day."
    Of course! In the Kingdom, every day is the first day, the original day of creation...

*   *   *

Friday, 10:30 am

    I am entirely responsible for my life. I am the only one responsible for any of it. There is no one else and nothing else to blame for anything that I experience.
    God, how I hate that part of self-empowerment!
    For years I've heard those statements as a kind of blanket blame: if I'm the only one responsible for my experience, then I'm the only one at fault when I don't like it. That's a lonely feeling. Especially when everyone I know is dancing at the Pity Party, slinging mud at parents, bosses, ex-wives, cheating husbands, and the government. Misery loves company...
    But if I want to be a creator, and to play with life instead of crying about it, then I have to take responsibility for everything that I create.
    Not because I'm looking to assign blame.
    But because I'm looking for the roots of power.

The principle is very simple: I either have the power to create the life I want, or I don't.

If I claim that I'm a victim in these circumstances, I deny my power. Without my power, I am stuck. Nothing can change, because the creator of change -- me! -- is powerless.

If I claim that I'm the one who made this mess, then with that proclamation I can grant myself the power and permission to undo it.

So, ugly and embarrassing as it may be, I've got to take responsibility for what I have created. I've got to own my whole experience, forgive myself for my mistakes, gather in my scattered and projected power, and put all that power to work.

Every moment is a new creation; every day's the First Day. A friend sent me a card I've hung up on the wall above my bed. It says: *"I FALL DOWN.*
         I GET UP.
         AND THE WHOLE TIME,
         I'M DANCING. "

*   *   *

Sunday evening

So in this perfect moment, in this first day of creation, what is it that I want to do? I've emptied myself out, set a match to my grandiose dreams, come back into my body, stumbling, dancing. I'm gathering my power, listening to my feelings. I'm determined to accept life as it is. Neither crushed nor defiant, I'm standing on my own. Without the Bungalows, without my family or friends, perhaps without JF, or money, or a job.

Small as I may be, small as my life is, I am here.

What do I want to do with this?

I ask myself the question Robert Fritz asks in The Path of Least Resistance: *"What do I love enough to want to bring to life?"*

It seems my sights have lowered, and I haven't got so much to work with any more. This cottage on the mountain, fog snaking shyly through the trees, raindrops clinging to my window. Memories of Hawaii, with its lava deserts and relentless sun. The friends and mentors who shared time and secrets with me. A warm house, with the cold gray world outside.

Rocking in my chair, my feet crossed on the sheepskin rug, wearing JF's woolen socks, and a sweatshirt left me by Jerome. Eggs boiling in the kitchen, a cup of steaming tea beside me on the desk, and everywhere, the muted grays of winter, fading into night.

Is this enough to interest anyone? My private world, the life I'm piecing together with love and luck and guesswork... Suddenly my life is very small.

As I look up from my reverie, I'm startled by my own reflection. Instead of trees and fog, I see my face. The window spread before me, backed by steam and darkness, has become a mirror.

When the outside disappears, when the great dreams vanish, what do I love enough inside myself to shepherd into life?

* * *

Monday, midnight

I want to become one with the world. I want all the walls between us to fall down. I want to reveal myself, nakedly, and be loved. I want to reach beyond all of my prejudices and judgments, and to embrace the world in all its wonder and horror; to feel my kinship with all living things, all living beings. I want every part of my world to come alive, and to celebrate the mystery and joy of life with me. I want all of us dancing, and shouting, and singing, from sheer amazing bliss.

I want to communicate this position through my writing, and to feel the YES! resonating in me so deeply I cannot resist surrendering to life, again and again and again. I want to sing with the angels, play poker with the devil, and be amazed at everything that lives.

I want to create a world beyond duality. I want to honor everything, be bound to nothing, love without ceasing, pray to the

God in every sliver of creation, and dance on my grave when I leave.

I want to be happy. I want to feel the full force of every emotion, every position, every drama and every freedom. I want to be so much alive that nothing else matters, that all these dreary issues and problems and fears become irrelevant. I want to be so big that I contain the world; I want to call creation back inside of me, spin it around, and laugh it out again.

I want to be one with God, and to know that God is one with me, and that all of us are living in that Oneness. I want to stop pretending that I'm miserable when the universe is singing and the trees are humming my name, and all of us are lovers, made for love and nothing less. I want all of us to be together, and to know it. I want nothing less than everything, and I want everyone to share it with me, open-armed and open-eyed and open-hearted...

* * *

Tuesday morning

This, then, is the new dream. A dream deep enough and big enough to warrant loving into life.

For this dream I'm willing to be humble; to give up my privacy and isolation; to share my feelings, without blaming anyone for them; to come back into the world instead of trying to transcend it; to be in my body, small and powerless as that may feel.

I've learned the hard way that the soul won't compromise. I can trick my mind, my body, and even my heart into believing they'll be satisfied with something less than wholeness. But the soul knows better.

No more will I choose between heaven and earth, between material success and spiritual riches. No more will I sell myself out for either one alone. I will find -- or forge -- a bridge between them both.

EMBRACING LIFE JUST AS IT IS

Monday evening

This morning I walked out to the road to pick up the mail and bring in the trash can. To my surprise, I felt a tinge of ownership, like I belonged here. This is my life. The gravel scrunched beneath my feet in a familiar way; the fog rolled up the hillside by its usual path. I waved goodbye to JF as he left for work, and said good morning to the crocus blossoms poking through the snow.

I've given up my inner journey. It seemed so powerful at first, but nothing on the outside changes. All my prayers and processing and affirmations haven't brought another dime into our bank accounts. All that power I've been generating can't do anything until I plug myself into the world. A thousand megawatts of electricity won't run a simple toaster till you plug the damn thing in.

This afternoon I set my writing down and took a hike. The hills around the house were clear-cut eighty years ago, but since then they've been undisturbed. Here and there are remnants of the old-growth forest, giant logs disintegrating into nurseries for newly sprouted seeds. Something in this spectacle of rot and healing soothes me. Nature's always building on the ruins.

Round a hill, or off through a break in the trees, the river sparkles. Inside the canopy of trees, the woods glow with the soft light of the mosses, and the almost phosphorescent rusts and reds of crumbling bark. The snow is nearly melted. Water trickles softly through the old stream beds.

I've found a new companion for my walks. Jeckyl, the golden retriever who lives across the street, comes to visit while his owners are at work. He loves to trot along when I head for the woods. Today he scampered through the puddles on the lower trail, lapping up the ice-cold water with delight.

When we got home, he plopped beside me on the deck, soaking up the waning sunlight. With a start, I saw the treasure map I'd made back in Hawaii. I've got everything I asked for.

* * *

Tuesday night, late

This afternoon I dug up my notes from the book. I tried to sketch the outlines of my talks with Kim and Peter, to feel them with me once again. For several hours I was living in two places at once, with volcanoes and palm trees mixed in with the local evergreens, and a swimming pool in the middle of the living room floor.

When I write about Hawaii, I lose track of where I am. No one ever told me it was such a physical sensation; I always thought that imagination is what happens inside your head, and when you open your eyes again, it's gone. Not so, at least not for me. When JF came home from work, he startled me. He opened the door, and walked right through the chair where Kim was sitting. It took me a moment to separate realities.

He didn't understand why I was shaking.

When you decide to live in more than just this one dimension, it's not easy to explain.

* * *

Thursday afternoon

I've been listening to a tape I made several years ago when I was in love. It starts and ends with Roy Orbison singing, "Anything you want, you got it!" Sandwiched in between are upbeat love songs filled with passion, tenderness and rapture.

I've started playing this tape everywhere, like a soundtrack for my life. I sing my love out to the dishes, the sky, the truck, the people passing on the street, Jeckyl as he tromps along beside me on the trails.

One morning I played it in the bathroom as I shaved. I caught my eye in the middle of an "I love you," and started singing to myself. That was powerful! The combination of music and words seems to hit both mind and emotions. It's much more fun than affirmations or emotional exercises.

One afternoon I was frustrated, and shook my body, trying to get loose. When the tape came on, I started dancing with myself. Now I've added physical movement to the mix, and the love songs sink in deeper.

As I clear away old patterns in myself, that creates some kind of emptiness, a vacuum waiting for new rhythms. Why not fill it up with songs of love?

*   *   *

Saturday

What is it that I lack?

I have a house to live in, food to eat, my health, work that I believe in, a friend to talk with, a dog to keep me company. Always wanting more is symptomatic of a deeply-rooted soul disease...

I read a question in Pure Wisdom *yesterday. "Do you have enough money for a month? A week? A day? An hour? A minute? A second? Find a time scale you can say 'enough' to."*

I practiced.

"Yes, for this minute, I have all I need."

"In this hour, nothing disastrous has happened."

"Today the bank did not foreclose."

Then I stretched the time line out into the future:

"We can buy groceries enough to last a week."

All of these experiences helped me open up a space in which to breathe. Even when I woke up in full money panic, I could always say:

"In this second, I am safe."

Getting in touch with that freedom, breathing in that moment of abundance, always disengaged the fears.

Never underestimate the power of "enough." To truly feel it, down into your core, is like the blasting of an atom...

- $ -

GOING OFF THE MONEY DRUG

JF came home early one evening. I'd been writing; my desk lamp was the only light on in the living room. He sank down into the shadows of the couch, exhaling in defeat. "I just can't do it anymore," he said. "When I'm making bucks, I can put up with all the bullshit. When there's no money, I can't get my heart into the work."

"Money is a drug," I replied, turning my chair. "I've noticed that since I stopped making it. Cold-turkey withdrawal clears your vision something fierce. Even a month ago, I craved it every day, believing if I only had another fix, I could survive."

"It's all that I can think about. When the bills get paid, and there's food in my belly, I'm still obsessed with the next fix." He looked up, miserably shaking his head.

"We're addicted. Welcome to America. Money is our God, and finance is the state religion. We visit our banks and shopping malls more often than we go to church. We worship the rich and famous as though they were divine. We hand our offerings to the financial priesthood, the bankers and brokers, and hope that they will intercede for us, in their infinite wisdom, with the Almighty Dollar."

"Money sucks."

"Money is a drug," I repeated. It felt good to have a handle on something again. I stood up from the desk and started pacing; my hands became more animated.

"Without money, there's no reason left to work. Sometimes money fuels and motivates us, like cocaine or coffee, stimulating us to new peaks of performance. Sometimes we use money, like alcohol or opium, to numb ourselves to pain and repetition. Money makes the suffering endurable.

"Whenever we use money as a drug, I think it masks an

underlying problem."

"What problem is that?" JF asked, half-heartedly. He was following my argument, but seemed unsure where it was leading.

"The problem isn't money; that's just a distraction." The hardwood floor creaked as I spun around to face him. "The real, true, original problem is work. Why do we need such a powerful drug to keep us working? Because working is unnatural."

"Yeah, right. So why does everyone do it?"

I stood before the window, lost in thought, gazing out across the city lights. When I spoke again, my voice was softer. "Because we've lost touch with the sources of abundance. We've sold away our power for some shiny golden promises. Once we've bought into the system, it's not hard to keep us strung along: car payments, families, mortgages, fancy new toys. Once we get started, the push is immense to keep doing what we're doing, for the money. We forget how to work for the joy of the working."

"There's joy in working?" He leaned forward, disbelieving. The light hit his face.

"Yes, if you're creating something that you value, if you're alive and playful." I sat down beside him. "Here's how I look at it: if you're a money addict, you consume; if you're a money magician, you create.

"Money addicts have to lie and cheat and steal to get another fix, because they can't create the resource on their own. All the power is outside of them.

"Money magicians travel inward to find their own source, their own power. It's a messy journey, to untangle all the lies, but once you do, you hold the keys to limitless creation."

He turned to face me. "So if you're a money magician, you don't make the money working."

"That's right. You make it playing."

"And if you're a money addict, the working itself is unimportant. It's only a means to an end."

"A boring, draining, self-defeating means."

"So why do we keep drudging along, and forgetting how to play?"

"Because the money's an addiction, and it covers up a deeper addiction."

"Which is..."

"The fear that we're unlovable. The false belief that we're imposters, and we might get caught. Leilani taught me how we all wear masks, pretending to be good and deserving, while we cover up our faults and guilt and doubts."

JF's breath was very shallow, as he sank back in the shadows. I continued.

"We perform our lives away, playing a role in someone else's script, because we're afraid to be ourselves. We work for other people, in jobs that don't suit us, so we won't have to take off our masks.

"Now that I am poor again, I see clearly how I've sold myself for money in the past. Every time I've been paid, in every job I've had, it's been because I've played a role successfully. At best, that means I've always been an actor; it also means I've been a whore. I've sold myself as a commodity.

"No matter how much money I've earned, what's valued isn't me, it's my performance. The underlying problem here is something money doesn't touch, and cannot heal.

"And so the money's never enough. Like any drug, it does the job, but always at a price, and always for a limited time. The more we use, the more we need. The approval is always conditional."

JF touched my knee, as a child might, and asked, "How could it be different?"

"You've heard of unconditional love?"

"Vaguely."

"It's a love that doesn't lay down laws or expectations. When I love you unconditionally, that means I love you always, under every circumstance, no matter what you do or don't do. I see past your mask, into your heart. I accept the contradictions and the ugliness inside you; I embrace the whole package. You don't have to dress it up for me.

"Unconditional love is like the love a parent feels for a child, eternal, open-ended. No matter what you put your parents through, no matter what you say or do with your life, you'll always have a direct line to their hearts. The bottom line, come hell or high water, is that you're ultimately loved."

JF, like most of us, still had some issues with his parents. "Sounds rare," he commented.

"Not so rare as you might think. It's often muddied by the ups and downs of daily life, by human fears and pettiness. But it will come out in a crisis, when there's been an accident or a loss, when we come face to face with what's truly important."

"I get it." He was engaged again. He pulled his feet up on the couch, and sat sideways. "So what does this have to do with work and money?"

"Let me go back to relationships for a minute. That might explain it better. Do you remember me talking about Mr. Pahrup, that Indian insurance guy at the Bungalows?"

"A little bit. What did he tell you?"

"He taught me about synergy. All of our relationships -- with parents, spouses, bosses, money, God -- are at heart the same. We're working out the same issues and needs, in a thousand different ways. So whatever we learn in one part of our lives may be of value in another area..."

"Yeah, I remember now. He said to apply your successes in one arena to your failures in another."

"Right. So I've been wondering about unconditional love, and money, and work. I don't have a mask to hide behind right now. Like it or not, I've been exposed. Now that the fog has lifted from my money addiction, and I am once again broke, I've had to think about going back to work."

"I've been wanting to talk to you about that."

"Not yet. Listen first. Now that my mask has been shattered, I've no desire to go back into that game. I'm willing to be exposed. In fact, I kind of like it. I feel relieved."

"You have been awfully chirpy lately."

"When you're not performing and pretending, life is rather fun. I have a lot more energy, now that I'm not always holding up that heavy mask. I can do what I please, now that I'm not trying to please someone else. And the scary part, the deliciously scary part, is that I'm improvising life, instead of following someone else's directions.

"I'm not interested in working for money any more. Oh, I want to have it, lots of it, but I'm not going to work for it again. Working people don't get rich."

"Then how will you make money?"

"By loving myself unconditionally, and learning to love money in exactly the same way. I know that real love can't be earned. If we have to work for it, then it's conditional. And when conditions change, that kind of love will disappear.

"Unconditional love is a gift that we don't have to earn, that we *can't* earn. It's a deep respect for who we really are, beneath the games and masks."

I shrugged and opened up my hands. "I believe that unconditional money must be the same. It can't be earned. It's a gift we give ourselves when we stop working for approval.

"Money is the prize in the financial realm, and like idiots, we're all working and cheating and stealing, trying to earn it, trying to win it. But LOVE CAN'T BE STOLEN OR EARNED! True love is not conditional, and neither is true wealth."

"But love and money aren't the same, David."

"How do we know that? Kim told me they were. I believe that love is energy, and money is a symbol for some kind of energy, and all energy flows by the same basic rules, like water downstream, or electricity through wires.

"When energy is in its solid form, it all looks different; but when it's moving, it's just energy. And energy flows where it's directed...

"I've never really let my money flow, because I've always treated it with fear and caution. I've never experienced unconditional money, because I've never dropped the masks and put myself out on the line.

"I do believe that I've stopped using money as a drug. All that ranting and raving I went through in the winter may have been withdrawal symptoms. Now that I am down to the next level, the level of work and earning, I want to love myself so deeply and completely that I never need that drug again..."

JF sighed, and leaned forward. "I want to break my money habit, too. But how can I stop working?"

"Maybe you're not ready for that step yet. Why not build up your strength in a different way? Once you learn to love yourself without conditions, maybe you can transfer that experience into the working world..."

I put my arms around him, and we hugged. Until we learn to do it on our own, sometimes it helps to share.

*   *   *

Most of us do money backwards. We believe abundance will come if we work hard, spend wisely, plan, save, and invest. That method rarely brings abundance. At best, it brings survival.

Survival focuses on not making mistakes: don't eat the poison berries, stay away from the edge of the cliff, hide when danger comes near.

Those of us who follow caution may live longer, but we won't experience the thrill and power of success. We won't experience the joy of oneness, or the peace of living unconditionally.

Success comes from discovering that there are greater gods than those who merely maintain life. There are the gods who make and break it, who destroy and create out of nothing...

As long as we live in survival consciousness, we're at the mercy of those greater gods. Our life is not ever our own. A market crash can sweep our life savings away, the earth can open underneath our feet...

When we decide to align with the gods of creation, the mold breaks, and the rules change. The cast comes off, and we can take our first steps toward wholeness.

This is not a book about survival.

This is a book about creating money out of nothing.

*   *   *

Wednesday night

My approach to money's changing. I'm descending into something more vast and much deeper than my usual financial affairs. Where I used to skitter on the surface -- worrying over a few bucks here or there, fretting over bills or jobs, or how to make it all work out -- now I've sunk below all that, into some strange new nether region.

Things move more slowly here; it's darker; and even though it's all unknown, it feels much safer and more grounded. There's definitely more power down here: I feel the movements of thousands and hundreds of thousands of dollars, almost in my guts. Must I let go of all the petty bills, in order to shift my focus onto something bigger? I can't seem to focus on both views at once: worry or safety, acceptance or fear. Which will I choose?

For the past few months, each bill has been paid as it's come due. JF's job has not improved, but I've begun attracting money from unusual and unexpected sources, in tiny dribbles, small amounts. New opportunities are coming up, and I'm pursuing them. I'm finding new ways to plug in.

I'm onto something magical. I hate to talk about it, for fear that I might somehow interrupt the flow. I don't really know how it works, or why.

Money isn't what it seems. Neither is work, or reward, or even play. When I connect with my deepest inner nature, in that place where life and I are one, I feel quite safe, even though I know a roller-coaster ride is coming up. In that Oneness, I let go of my personal desires and demands, surrender them to life, and they come back to me fulfilled.

And so I'm moving into a suspended state of grace, slowly learning the practice of amazement and of gratitude. Worrying over money and work distracts me from appreciating what's in front of me. I've decided to release my fears, refusing to be limited by appearances. I've decided to trust life. It's time to open and unfold...

The other night, I filled the tub with water, and quietly stepped in. After I'd rested in the darkness for a while, I floated three lit candles on the water's surface. The candlelight bobbed gently out over the void: that fragile bobbing was exactly how I felt inside. The candles themselves hung suspended; I watched their shadows move across the floor of the tub. This is my life, I thought. A light hanging out in the darkness, with no visible means of support.

I believe that anyone can move into this state of grace, though most of us choose not to because the stakes are too high: we must forfeit our personal lives and desires. We must surrender our survival fears, our obsession with status and money. The ego cannot enter here; it is too big to fit through the door. Only the humble, who release all sense of self, can turn sideways and disappear through the door no one can see.

Here in this subterranean darkness, I trust and allow. Money flows, and grace flows, and healing and love flow, wherever they are allowed to go. Only our walls and separations keep them out. It's just that simple.

When I let down my barriers to money, when I eliminate my fears and judgments and demands, money will flow into the space I have created, to the degree that I am willing to accept it. When I let down my barriers to grace, and healing, and love, they will also flow toward me.

I move into the consciousness that all of life and I are one, and trust that we are creating something real and magical. When I let go of my own will, the world is very simple. And, to my constant surprise, that world seems to be filled with abundance and love.

- $ -

A JOB MADE IN HEAVEN

Monday afternoon

I've started playing a new game with life. I call it "Deaf and Dumb." I pretend that God is on the far side of a soundproof glass: He can see me clearly, but we cannot hear each other. If I stand in one place, moving my lips, God will think I'm happy there, and support me in continuing that activity. If I start to move in a direction, life will flow around me to support that movement. All my words are useless; only actions count.

Changing my mind does nothing more than change my mind: it generates new thoughts. Changing my heart does nothing more than generate new feelings. I can change my beliefs and my attitudes all day long, and all I'll get for my troubles is new beliefs and a fresh attitude. Those changes may be great, but they won't have very much effect on physical reality.

Life can't support concepts; it needs tangible actions. The energy needs somewhere material to flow, something physical to activate. And so, I'm trying to direct the abundance into some channels. I'm trying to create a new kind of job for myself, a job based on joy.

* * *

For years, I'd searched for new jobs based on what I had already mastered, the work experience and skills of the past. Because my work was all just a performance, it was easier to repeat variations on the same old role. What I did on one stage, for one audience, I could do on another. This kept me trapped in the same line of work.

But that spring, as I dipped my toes back in the working

world, I wanted something different. I'd lost all interest in repeating the habits and successes of the past. And so, I was thrown back onto different resources.

What did I love to do? What was so obvious and easy that I always overlooked it? I spent hours digging deep into myself, searching for clues, bringing up buried treasures which I've always covered over or discounted.

My strongest resource seemed to be my self-awareness. Since my breakdown, and my constant days and nights of journaling, I'd discovered how to get down to the heart of things.

To my surprise, I found that I could turn this same awareness onto others. To some, this appeared magical. To me, it was simply a matter of paying attention.

When I pay attention to people, I can process a lot of information very quickly. Who you are and what you feel is visible on many levels: in your face, the way you hold your hands, the words you choose and the sound of your voice. Once I take off my mask, I can more clearly see through yours.

Leilani once said that anyone who doesn't buy into your mask -- an animal, a child, an enemy, a sorcerer -- will see the whole of you. I want to know the whole of you. I want to see into the heart.

Some call this skill intuition. Some say I can tell the future. Some call me a counselor and healer.

Writing this book, even back then, was opening my imagination and increasing my awareness. An unexpected side effect was that the deeper I went into myself, the deeper I could go into others.

I would meet someone, and immediately know depths inside them which they rarely knew themselves, at least not in words. From the richness of the present moment I'd extrapolate a plot, a story about who they were and where they were going. When those stories resonated, people began crying or sighing in relief. Their lives made sense!

I was onto something here.

It was a bit unnerving for most people when I just started spouting off these stories about them. They seemed to be more comfortable if we used a format. Sometimes I would ask them to make a drawing, and we'd look at that. Years ago, when I was working in her school, my friend Barbara taught me how to read pictures with kids. Pictures are a straight connection to the heart.

Sometimes I'd haul out a deck of intuitive cards I have used with myself and a few close friends for many years. When we played this game, the stories I told seemed to have some concrete basis. At least the cards were real.

And so, I started doing consultations for a wider circle of friends. Joyce brought me out to the preschool where she works, and I read drawings for the kids. Someone talked me into working at a psychic fair one day at a local bookstore, and that led to other invitations. Once a week I went out to a coffee shop in Hillsboro, and did mini-sessions at a table in the back. Heart readings, I called them. Soul x-rays.

I started making pocket money. It wasn't much, but at least JF and I could go out to the movies once in awhile, or buy ourselves new shoes.

Best of all, it was free money. It didn't cost me anything to make: I just did what I would love to do anyway, and then asked someone to pay me. It was coming to me without any effort. And it helped me clarify the processes I was playing with in my own life.

I didn't advertise, or seek out customers. I just went where I was invited, and talked about what's real. I didn't write myself a resume, or interview for someone else's job description. In the real world, when you're selling water in the desert, no one asks to see your license and credentials.

I discovered a great secret: when I drop my mask, and speak from the heart, life responds.

- $ -

ROADS NOT TAKEN

Spring was in full bloom; the land was lush with flowers. One day while JF was at work, I drove out to the country to visit Joyce. It was hard to focus on the road: my eyes were drawn along the streams, between the trees, off on the mountainsides. The fields from one horizon to the next were clouded with daisies and dandelions, iris and bachelor's buttons.

Joyce and I went picking wild rosebuds down by the creek. The open flowers, gently scented, were a delicate white, blushing at the edges with color; but the younger rosebuds clenched themselves excitedly into a vibrant, shocking pink. They screamed with color, like entire symphonies locked in a single note.

I hopped across the creek, and started picking from the far side of the thicket. Water burbled underneath us, hidden by the canopy of leaves and flowers. We stuffed our pockets, and filled several baskets; always, there was more.

Joyce intended to make leis with these tight pink buds, and to sell them at a women's gathering she went to every summer. She had her own intense connection with their power. One spring she had conceived in a moment of rapture, and later miscarried the child.

As she moved through her grief, mourning what was lost forever, she found an alternate emotion welling up: the desire to honor the brief life which had lived inside of her, the unborn baby girl. The contradictory emotions of sadness, acceptance, and celebration all wove together into a single experience, and that weaving made a perfect circle. A lei.

Each spring, Joyce gathered wild rosebuds. These buds were plucked while they were still ripe with potential and life, and strung together into circles. For her, these rosebud leis were a way of remembering, and honoring the little girl who never had a chance to fully bloom.

After she had shared this story, we picked quietly, lost in our own private thoughts. A light Oregon mist had settled on the valley, and gradually, without really noticing it, we got wet. The gentle rain felt like a blessing, another outpouring of life and nature's bounty. Eventually my private thoughts spilled over into words.

I'd never considered before that each dream, each vision, each seed has a right to be appreciated for itself, and honored on its own terms. Not every action needs to be a steppingstone to something bigger and better. As I've focused on goals and success in my life, I've become relentless in discounting whatever isn't bearing fruit for me. I was stunned by Joyce's celebration of the child she lost. How much do I miss by only focusing on what pays off?

As I work and play my way toward unconditional living and love, I might begin relationships which only last for hours, or weeks. Who knows what we have to learn together, what we have to share? I've been told to treat each person that I meet as the bearer of a gift especially for me; it's my job to discover and unwrap the gift that's hidden in the person. How many times do I casually toss out the package, gift unopened, when I decide this person and I have no future? Not every seed bears fruit which I can recognize; sometimes nourishment can come from unfamiliar sources.

In the world of work, I might take on projects or jobs which lead nowhere. I might spend countless hours setting up a dream which then falls through. It's important not to judge that time, or the dream which inspired that labor. If nothing else, I've learned to pour more of myself into my work. Everything I do is valid; everyone I meet has value.

Along the way to unconditional abundance, there are many false starts and dead ends. Most of the species which have ever lived on earth are now extinct. Nature is extravagant with her creations; every acre of land teems with billions of seeds which will never sprout and blossom. Still, look at these hills, lush with wildflowers! If nature moaned and wailed about every seed which never made it, she'd be too exhausted to support the few seeds which will ultimately grow.

Can I learn to constantly create, and constantly surrender my creations; dream and then scatter my dreams to the wind? Sometimes a seed will have a different purpose than I might expect; I must be willing to make room for magic in my process, room for miracles. I must also be willing to make room for dead ends, and projects which die on the vine. Can I be big enough to risk a lot of failures, in order to ensure a few successes? Can I emulate nature, and completely love each dream I want to live, whether or not it ever comes to be?

Men and women have distinctly different approaches to creation. While we worked toward the center of the thicket, Joyce and I shared how biology affects our basic attitudes toward life. Women nurse a single egg each month; then hold the embryo, the single dream, in utero for nine long months. Men produce twelve million sperm an hour. To conceive, a woman holds and pulls in energy; men release and scatter.

I'd been taught to build my dreams with female energy, to focus and nurture and choose, to eliminate alternatives. I'd been taught to make priorities, to pour all my attention into one career, one project. But true male energy creates in very different ways: through variety, and juggling many deals at once, and always generating new ideas.

Most of the projects I've started have fizzled out or crashed before they ever reached maturity. For many years I took that personally, as a sign of failure, and tried to minimize my future risks.

Back when I was living in the harsh, cold winter, this strategy made sense. With limited resources, and limited energy, it pays to choose your battles wisely.

Now that I was surrounded by the abundance of spring, I reconsidered my plans. So what if something fell through? So what if some seeds banged into walls, or got lost under rocks? There were always more ideas, more inspirations, more projects to try. If I was endlessly inventive and creative, my failures wouldn't matter. Only when I hedged my bets, and tried to hold on, could I lose.

As we picked rosebuds that day, sharing losses and lessons, we also talked about abundance. In that setting, it was hard to feel poor: life poured out gifts almost more quickly than we could receive them.

I talked about how much has changed in my life these past few months: I'm now working for myself, making my own schedule, doing what I love. Sometimes I'm ashamed that my attitude seems several steps behind reality; so often as I cruise down the highway of life, I'm messing around in the back seat with fear, instead of enjoying the road or the wonders I'm driving through.

Being in the country, amidst all these wildflowers, gave me a chance to catch up with the truth. Joyce was really into celebrating the abundance; she helped me shift toward gratitude.

When we first began to gather the rosebuds, I felt sorry that they'd never reach their full potential. As I worked with them and talked, I came to understand that every gift has many uses. If I insisted that they bloom and mature there, on the side of the road in the rain, I'd deny those rosebuds the chance to become a part of Joyce's healing, or mine, or perhaps of your own.

Who knows where the road will take them once they've been released by our plucking? Lovers may wear them, or sisters. They may become gifts at a graduation, or a funeral. Someone may drape these rosebuds over a lampshade, and in the cold of winter, they will remember spring. Not every dream has to flower.

And not every flowering will follow the direction we expect; sometimes, seeds flower years later, or in different dimensions. The roses I picked on that spring day with Joyce are still blooming in the pages of my heart; and now those same seeds I am passing on to you.

That evening, as I helped Joyce string those rosebuds into leis, I honored all the false starts and aborted dreams I had conceived in my lifetime. I honored all the tries and misses, all the failures and forgotten friends. They helped to make me what I am today. As I strung those rosebuds into leis, I celebrated all the mixed emotions which come with life, and making life, and giving myself over to life.

Out there in the flow that day, slipping in and out of the creek, gathering roses in the Oregon drizzle, I had participated in a ceremonial detour from my goal-obsessed life. Those rosebuds couldn't bring me one step closer to achieving any of my goals. And yet their seeds were not wasted: somewhere in me they are germinating still.

* * *

Other seeds were ripe, and ready to explode that week. I soon discovered that not all of them were flowers.

Trouble was brewing between JF and me. The more I got involved with working elsewhere, the more agitated he became that I wasn't writing the book.

When JF began supporting me, we settled into old, familiar roles. In the financial realm, he had control. Sometimes he acted like a jealous husband, threatened when his wife wanted to work outside the home. He had mixed feelings about supporting me: pride, anger, fear that this would never end.

I resented that I'd given so much power to him, and become so helpless. To balance things out, I played wise father to his lost little boy. In the spiritual realms, I was the master. We drove each other to extremes, fighting to restore some sort of balance.

One evening, during a truce, we went downtown to see a movie. While we were gone, the truck, parked on a side street, was vandalized.

JF first noticed that the window had been smashed. By the time I got a good look at the hole where the stereo should be, he'd already taken off for the corner, stalking the downtown street for suspects. Whoever ripped it out must have had problems: a thin trail of blood ran from the window to the floor. I leaned back against the open door and shook my head.

"Call the cops!" he shouted back at me.

"What for? The damage is already done."

But he was in a fighting mood, and took it out on me.

"Don't you give a shit? What's wrong with you?"

I sat down, shaking, on the curb. The primal sense of being violated had propelled us in two different directions: he, toward pointless action, and me, toward pointless emotion. I might as well run through the feelings, I had told myself. Nothing we can do tonight will bring our stereo back.

But it took a phone call to the police, a seven-minute wait on hold, and the promise that they'd send the necessary paperwork -- by mail! -- before JF switched gears. No one would be coming out to take our report at the scene; no one would be caught. He kicked a lightpost and cursed; I retreated into shuddering silence. The split between us magnified as we drove up the hill toward home.

"This isn't working," I finally said as he turned the corner onto Skyline. Trees whistled by in the dark.

"What? Oh, forget about it; I'll get the window fixed tomorrow."

"I don't mean the window. I mean us, together. Our styles are just too different. I need to find another way to do this project."

"You mean the book?"

"I mean the book. You're not happy; I'm not happy. I don't feel the love behind this partnership. We're always on edge."

"So what do you want to do about it?"

"I want to cancel our agreement. I want to get out and start making some serious money again."

He exhaled sharply in the dark.

"What about our deal?"

"I still want to write, but not full time. It's going to take energy to get an income started."

I could feel the release, a strange mixture of relief and fear. "What happens next?"

"I don't know. I'm making this up. Do you want to help?"

"I'm not sure how," he admitted. "But I'm willing to try."

- $ -

AN INTERACTIVE GAME

For several weeks, I played with generating services and products. How many ways could I create to be real? Instead of following a single path, I let my imagination go wild. I wrote a pamphlet, started a class, continued my intuitive conversations. I threw handfuls of seeds to the wind.

There was always the temptation to define myself in someone else's terms, or to join a team, or to work for somebody else. Sliding into precast concrete, I called it. Easy at first, but ultimately limiting.

For the moment, I jealously guarded my power. Instead of listening to other people, spouting old advice and prejudices, I went directly to the source. I didn't want anyone else deciding what was possible for me. I wanted to play in the moment, to interact with each new day, to let life itself show me what was and wasn't possible.

*   *   *

Friday, 2:15 pm

When I slow down, life flows. The world softens, like putty in my hands: it's malleable, I can shape it. Life has tendencies, not laws. Nothing's hard and finished.

When I speed up, the world becomes more solid. Maybe this is just a quality of motion. If I step into a lake, I sink right down into the water. When I'm pulled up by a boat to waterski, barreling along, the water seems as hard as concrete. It resists.

In that solid, moving world, money is "out there." The faster I chase it, the more obvious it seems that it really is out there. Assumptions have their own momentum: they're self-

fulfilling prophecies. If I expect life to be hard, it will usually oblige me.

So when I'm out chasing money, the very act of chasing reinforces my beliefs that money must be chased, because it's sure not in my grasp, it keeps slipping away. This fuels my desire to continue the chase, because I must be getting closer, I've invested so much energy already...

Today, I will slow down. I want to play with life instead of working at it. I want to sink down into the refreshing water, to feel money all around me, to trust that the money's unlimited, that it's within my grasp.

I want to cultivate my creativity.

I know that creativity is a very different state of mind than racing through the world to catch what seems outside of me. I'm coaxing into being something which has never existed before; I'm reaching inside myself to pull out something new.

This requires a different rhythm, a different method than the ones I use to reap the harvest of the world. I'm not picking or packaging or selling someone else's product. I'm learning how to grow my own.

Edith Piaf, the great French singer, had this to say about success: "Don't cover up your faults; they may turn out to be your greatest strengths. They make you unique, and irreplaceable. Anyone, with enough practice and desire, can learn to sing perfectly. But only those who cultivate their flaws will melt your heart."

I want to play the money game like that.

* * *

Monday evening

This new "career" is taking off. Two separate bookstores want my help as they launch new publications; there's fan mail on my answering machine; and a class full of people have signed up to do a Dream Circle with me.

I took a piece I'd written in Hawaii in a fever one week-

end, and put it into booklet form. Down at the local copy center, I xeroxed fifty copies, then stapled them together into books. Beyond Meditation *is now on bookstore shelves (at least in the bookstores where I do my intuitive consultations). Jenean, who owns the coffee shop in Hillsboro, has sold a dozen copies in the last few weeks. She says it made her cry...*

I can hardly focus on the money book. It seems like a project from lifetimes ago. I know I need to get back to it, but right now I can't concentrate. I'm too busy creating abundance to write about it!

*   *   *

Tuesday morning

The old rules are dropping away. They peel off my life like the skin slips off a baked tomato: simply, without effort. I go deeper inside. Distractions fall away. There are many seeds here. Juice drips down my chin.

Money flows. Without working, from some karmic reservoir, what I've earned, what's owed me, steadily flows in. Unexpected checks arrive. The less I pay attention to my fears and obligations, the more I'm paid.

Opportunities come out of nowhere. Unexpected, unbelievable. The phone rings, over and over. There's labor involved, energy expended, but the money still keeps flowing. More than ever. This is how it goes.

I'm not resisting. I deserve this. It no longer seems strange, or strained. The more I let go, the more this process flows.

I am doing my work, preparing the ground for planting and harvest. It's all coming back: not just money, but memories, states of consciousness, grace. My sharing gets deeper and simpler. I'm not afraid anymore.

I keep on doing what's in front of me. Flip the switches, open up to receive, reclaim my power. I'm plugging up the points of leakage. Power stops draining away, and flows back into me.

Just like money. And wisdom. And peace.
I'm harnessing the Sun.
I'm on track.
I'm aligned.

*   *   *

Friday, 2:30 pm

An article I sent to The New Times *in Seattle has been published.* "Spiritual Economics" *must have struck a nerve. It was accepted immediately, and placed on page one. This week, I got four long distance calls from strangers wanting to speak with the author. I mentioned I was writing a book,* Unconditional Money, *and three of them wanted to know where to buy it.*
Nice feedback.
This morning, out of the blue, I got a letter from my life insurance company, informing me that I had built up several hundred dollars in collateral with them. I have the choice of selling out the policy, or borrowing against it.
Last week I got a check from a dear relative, a close friend of my grandmother, who'd heard through my mom that I'd taken time off to write, and was a little low on money.
When you send it out, it comes back. It just doesn't always come back in the way we first expect. I sent out an article, which got printed in Seattle. I got paid by a relative in the Mid-west, and an insurance company from California.
How many times have I waited by the mailbox for a letter which was inside sitting on my kitchen table? Sometimes the mail has already arrived...
I've expected certain people to repay my kindnesses to them, when they were long gone or oblivious to what I'd done. And yet, while I was waiting (and usually feeling sorry for myself), someone else might pop up to return the favor. As they politely knocked on the front door, I realized how many times I was fuming out back, and didn't hear them!
Life doesn't pay much attention to methods; it just flows through whichever channel's easiest. To life, we're all the same,

like fingers on a single hand. If you were reaching to pick something up, and one hand was full, you'd use the other without even thinking. It's that way with life: if one of us is busy or preoccupied, the energy will move in through a stranger, a distant relative, or even an insurance agency. Life's not prejudiced or partial.

The instant we step out of ego, we are welcome to experience the constant flow.

- $ -

THE EGGSHELL CRACKS OPEN

Thursday, nearly midnight

All the walls are coming down. I actually let myself feel "falling in love": with life, with nothing in particular, with everything at once. How hard it is to be willing to love, to be totally open and vulnerable! How hard it is to trust that life can love me back, that someone or something out there can respond to the passion I feel in my heart...

Yet yesterday I did just that. I entertained the feeling that it was safe for me to let go and trust life! It's hard to say that without exclamation points. Such an incredible rush! Now that I'm out here so far, and I've given up so much stability and security, and I'm putting my dreams on the line, it's even tougher in some ways. And yet, I need to trust if I'm going to get any farther...

This is all happening in a very physical and grounded way. It's pure sensation and emotion, energy rushing through my body.

My relationships help to open up the private and closed places I protect inside myself; and while I'm out there, hanging to the wind, I let the love start flowing, and suddenly I realize that I'm healing more than just the misunderstanding of the moment, more than whatever silly issue I've been arguing about. I'm healing my relationship with life, and with myself. The blocks begin as problems in one particular relationship, and run much deeper. So when I "solve" them here and now, the healing goes much deeper too.

I didn't realize how scared I am right now, and how scared I've always been, that I'm unlovable, that for some reason life won't support me, that I'm alone and ultimately responsible for my own life, that if I don't protect myself and fight to be alive, somehow I'll be swallowed by cosmic indifference and uncaring humanity.

It gets muddy in there, but the general impression seems to be that I'm alone, and no one else, including God, really cares.

In my mind, I'm often able to talk myself into other positions, but somehow those reassurances don't sink all the way down into my guts. I guess that's why I need to go through personal relationships, so I can get all the way down there.

What a miracle it is to finally allow <u>believing</u> to soak into my body. How strange and wonderful to consider again that living is a risk worth taking. It's a privilege just to be at the gambling table, to be able to take the biggest risk of all. I'm falling in love with life; I feel it in my fingers, I feel it in my toes...

* * *

Saturday morning

While I've been out falling in love with life, JF and Joyce have been, more practically, falling in love with each other. I wondered what was going on with them; they've both been busy a lot lately.

I got the news last night. Now that I'm not working on the book, JF wants to move on. I guess I asked for this.

I guess JF has found his way to practice love again. It's too abstract for him to fall in love with life, or money. I must remember: we start with where we're at. Once we feel the feeling of loving unconditionally, we can apply it anywhere.

It will be a test for me to apply it to them...

Joyce is spinning. She's trying to stay open to us both. We all have spent a lot of time together; she and I have history.

They want to live together, in the country. JF says he'll still support me, but I know that won't be happening. He'll try, but I doubt he can find decent-paying work that far away from town.

Maybe he'll give up working for a living. I'd like him to get off the money drug -- even if he <u>is</u> my safety net.

He has agreed to pay the rent before he leaves; it's up to me to come up with the other bills and car payments. At the rate I'm going, I can handle that.

He and Joyce are cleaning up the house out in the country, on the farm her sister bought, where Joyce and I picked rosebuds. They sound busy, and exhausted, and excited for the future.

* * *

Saturday night

Falling in love amplifies every emotion. Living on the edge brings up my deepest fears. It's like turning up the volume on the stereo: everything gets louder. The highs and lows, the trebles and basses, the ballads and the screeching guitars. The volume dial doesn't differentiate; it cranks up everything equally.

When I allow myself to fall in love, every moment becomes heightened. I have to expect that if angelic choruses increase, so will demonic backbeats. Can you feel them down there in the floorboards, reverberating? More love brings up more fear.

If I want to turn up the bliss in my life, if I want to create more abundance, I've got to be willing to deal with more sorrow and loss. Whatever I have numbed inside myself will come up to the surface, wailing. The moment I decide to open up my eyes and ears, I will encounter everything I've been avoiding...

* * *

Shortly after that, JF moved his things out. That first night alone, before I went to sleep, I had to close the closet door. Those empty hangars and bare shelves reminded me that no one else was coming home. All night long I woke up, sweating, at the slightest sound.

I started finding excuses to go out. I couldn't bear to be alone. One evening while I was away, Nicole called from Hawaii. She left a simple message: her mother had died and was being buried outside Paris that Saturday morning.

For Nicole, at the other side of the world, it would be Friday evening at 11:00 when the lid on her mother's casket was finally closed. She was going to drop some flowers into the ocean then. Would I take a moment at that time to say a prayer for Mamie?

I remembered her mother. When I stayed with them in Paris, I had given her *"le plus grand massage des pieds"* -- the best foot rub -- she had ever had. She was a simple country woman, always on her feet, always working and cleaning. Every day she spent hours cooking heavenly meals for the family.

Her husband died a year ago, and Mamie had grown tired of living. When I closed my eyes on Friday evening, I saw her circling near the bottom of a whirlpool of stars, as though she were too heavy to rise up. She'd become saturated with loneliness, like a sponge full of tears. She kept looking down toward the earth, afraid to let go.

I pointed up, where I could feel a host of old friends and family waiting for her. She smiled sadly at me and continued to hover just over the planet, as though she were looking for something.

Saturday afternoon, I called Nicole back to tell her my story and ask about hers.

Two weeks ago, she told me, she'd awakened on a Sunday morning, with the strongest feeling that she had to go back home. She called and talked to Mamie, who said that everything was fine. For some reason, Nicole still felt compelled to go.

Monday morning she found a discount plane ticket, and called the hotel to tell them she wouldn't be in. A lot of people there weren't happy with her snap decision, but by Monday evening she was on her way to Paris.

She had a marvelous week with her mother. Nicole confessed that she had been writing down memories from her childhood, "nothing that would mean anything to anyone but me," about cooking with her Mamie, the sunlight in the woods outside her town, the smells at the sausage vendor down the street, handmade lace on a favorite dress, playing ball with her brother. All these scraps had been recorded, night after night, in one of those blank books you buy in a gift store. When she went home to visit, she'd taken this book along with her. Her mother laughed and cried over these stories as they read them together. "But these are all good," she'd protested. "What about the awful times?"

Mamie was sure she'd done something horrible to drive her only daughter so far away. "I don't remember them, but just for you, I'll try," Nicole had promised. "I'll write them up for you and bring them with me next time."

When she got back to Hawaii, she set the book on her night table. Three days later, she got the call that Mamie had died of a heart attack. They found her on the kitchen floor, with dinner burning on the stove, and the house filled with smoke.

Nicole had no money or time to return for the funeral. She'd already done what she could do, and there were other family members to take care of things for now.

Being Parisian has its price. Nicole has a natural elegance that often rubs people the wrong way; it doesn't help that she is also a perfectionist. If the truth be told, Nicole's not the most popular manager at the hotel. The guests invariably love her, but the busboys cringe when she walks by. She never lets them get away with anything; her standards are too high.

Word got around, as word will do, that Nicole's mother had died. Someone at the hotel found out about the funeral; someone else asked why she'd brought a basket of freshly-picked flowers to work. By the time 11:00 o'clock rolled around, everyone at the hotel had heard that Nicole was taking those flowers to the beach to bid aloha to her mother.

At the end of the dinner shift, still dressed up in her fancy clothes, Nicole slipped out a side door, left her shoes, and made her way down to the beach in the dark. A small crowd of people had already gathered on the shore. Most of them were carrying flowers, some picked from bushes around the hotel, some from their gardens at home. She even saw a busboy she had scolded just that afternoon, with a handful of flowers he had grabbed from a table arrangement in the dining room.

Friends and enemies alike had come to wish her mother

bon voyage. They fell in line behind her as she led the way down to the sea, with shaking footsteps and a bursting heart. At the water's edge, she stepped into the surf and tossed her flowers to eternity. Out of the darkness, dozens of hands did the same.

The sky rained flowers. The surf came to carry them away. Like a distant church bell through the night, she heard Leilani's voice erupting in an old Hawaiian mourning song.

The night filled with voices; voices rose and fell in waves around them. The stars and sea and rocks joined in, called together by this tiny human family. On a rock in the middle of the ocean, thousands of miles from the home where she was born, Nicole felt Mamie moving through her. In this foreign land she had adopted, Nicole could feel her mother's presence.

The others all felt something like a bird, swooping through the darkness, riding the waves of their song, something soft and fragile and no longer earthbound, like the flowers that were riding out to sea. "It was the talk of the hotel," Nicole assured me. "You know they love a good ghost story."

I told her how I'd seen her mother, circling, close to earth, refusing to go up.

"Mamie was looking for us," she said simply. "That was why she couldn't go. When Leilani started singing, and all those flowers touched the sea, she found us. I am glad you stayed by her. *Merci beaucoup, mon cher.* Was she glad to see you?"

I would have said *Yes*, and *thank you* too, but I couldn't get the words out through my tears.

- $ -

SOMETIMES I FEEL
LIKE A MOTHERLESS CHILD

Saturday, sometime

When I was a child, everything was taken care of for me. I never knew where it came from, or how: food appeared on the table, magically; clean clothes were always in the dresser drawers; we had a house to play in when the weather got cold, and when the sun came out, we skipped into the yard, or out onto the street. When I got tired, I slept, or fussed until someone put me to bed. Someone always came when I needed help, with a scraped knee or a homework problem.

Now that I am grown, I know how all that came to be. My parents conspired to create for me a magic kingdom in which all my needs were always met.

Now that I am grown, my parents aren't here. JF and Joyce are gone. I have to do it for myself. When I lie awake at night, I wonder if Nicole is also feeling lost...

I'm out here on the edge, alone, without a safety net. No, that was yesterday. Today, with a single strand of consciousness to hold me up, I've jumped. I'm over the edge, halfway into the physical world, feet dangling, spinning in the wind, my rope caught somewhere I can't see.

There is no comfort here for me. I'm halfway in my body. My only company is a screaming, frightened inner child. He wants constant reassurance, and there is none. Apparently he's lived alone in this body of mine, abandoned and neglected, powerless, for years. I don't know how to deal with him. When the operation seems most critical, when the rope is fraying or the gear gets stuck -- just when I most need to concentrate -- he loses his cool and starts wailing.

My friends are gone, and I am all alone.

New friends don't know what to do with me. They love to talk about love, but when the cards are on the table and I say, "here, now, in this body," they freak. I've passed some comfort zone, violated some trust. The social contract says that we won't bring love down into our bodies.

My feelings don't fit into the tidy boxes which we use to build up the foundations of our lives: marriage, commitment, safety, monogamy, that "special someone." What I'm discovering, out here over the edge, is that love isn't special; it's as free and common as the air. Love isn't something you can lock up into a relationship. It's a state of being, a quality of openness.

When I open my heart, I'm in love. Period. With everything, with everyone. I may choose to focus on one particular person; I may decide to share my body in the act of love with certain people, and not with others. But those are behaviors. Actions. What I do with the air. No matter how I use the air, it's still everywhere, it still completely saturates this world.

When I was a little boy, I remember the teacher once saying that God is everywhere. Being young and literal, I imagined God under the bed, in the dresser drawers, inside the shoe in the shoebox, hiding in the darkness of my closet. There is nowhere God is not, she said. In the freezer, at the bottom of the ocean, inside jellyfish, in the thermos in my lunchbox.

Now I'm learning that, just like that omnipresent God, love is everywhere. In my darkest secrets, in my shame, in every emotion, every twisted thought. Love is even living in my body! Love lives in my desires, my failures and successes; love even lives in money!

There's nowhere love is not.

Which seems to bring me into conflict with the boundary-makers. That's why I'm perceived as being "over the edge." The simple act of being in my heart and in my body puts me out beyond the normal boundaries!

On the old medieval maps, the flat world ended out at sea, and "there be monsters." Someone pushed those boundaries, broke through those fears, and brought back word that there were also untold riches and treasures to be found.

So far, I can say that's true about the new worlds I'm exploring. But every level I encounter brings another set of dragons. Every step I take into the material realms exposes me to older, deeper fears. The little boy I'm finding in my body, shivering and lonely, has few survival skills. He's helpless and demanding. He craves love and physical connection like someone stranded in the desert, dying of thirst.

I discovered similar layers of neediness and fear when I first broke through into my feelings. I'd hoped that when I leaped off the cliff into the physical, my challenges would be less emotional. Not so. They're still saturated with emotion, with the added weight of being physical, too. Density on top of density...

All because I decided to find God in money. All because I wasn't willing to live in an artificial human version of reality; because I wanted to know what life was like beyond our limited conceptions, beyond the layers and layers of programming we've all received about money and love and our bodies and the world we live in.

See, when I go into my mind, I can find the orderly thoughts that make sense of all this. But when I'm out there dangling in my body, all I know is chaos and abandonment. The only voice I hear is that screaming three-year old, wondering where everybody's gone to, why they've left him all alone. That three-year-old is not equipped to deal with the vast world of matter all on his own. Yet, so far, he seems to be the only guide out here who knows the territory at all...

No wonder no one comes out this far into money or love. Out here, we're all broken-down, abandoned children, living among the shattered ruins of our individual childhoods, limited by what we've learned, trying to find our ways across vast continents with only faded scraps of ancient maps to guide us...

*   *   *

Sunday

I'm here. This is what's happening. I've got to stop crying, stop looking around for someone to rescue me. The only person in this place who can take care of me is me.

I must become a parent, like it or not, ready or not. There is a little boy here screaming; someone must assume responsibility.

I'm cleaning out the wound. It's deep, and festering; it must be broken open, scrubbed clean, disinfected. Someone has to take charge, do the dirty work, be firm, not cave in to the pain.

This is how the body heals; the same steps hold true for the heart, and for the soul. When I make a new decision -- to be healed instead of wounded, to be whole instead of broken -- that decision happens in an instant.

But the healing process takes its own sweet time.

After I clean out a physical wound, the body swings into action: pus builds up, skin tightens and scabs over. There may be fever, inflammation. Toxins ooze up to the surface.

Finally, the actual repair begins. Skin is mended, veins sewn back together, new cells are created. The wholeness that I first envisioned takes hold in my body, and in physical reality.

It helps me to remember those steps. They are the same in the body, the heart, and the soul.

When I first ask for healing, I often get pain. Pain is not a punishment; it's a sign that energy is finally moving in the wound. When my leg has fallen asleep, and the blood first starts flowing again, all I feel is pins and needles. It's important not to give up at that point. If I do, I sabotage the healing process I've been praying for.

- $ -

DANCING ON THE RAINBOW BRIDGE

Morning

Breathing in, I greet my body.
Breathing out, I greet the day.
My body feels tight, and slightly nauseous.
Breathe into it.
I don't like to feel this way. I didn't know that I would find this when I finally let go. I've lost all my security. No job, no friends, no money, no partner. Every time I breathe, I feel the trauma. David is bleeding, and I don't know how to take care of him.

I blame my parents for their unfinished parenting, but the truth is that they're not alone. I don't have a clue how to heal this little boy. No one here on earth feels capable; everyone's reverting to the wounded inner child. We are a planetful of children...
Breathing in, I feel my body.
Breathing out, I feel my pain.
JF and Joyce are children, too, guessing their way through life, doing what they can. How strange it feels to go from such deep intimacy, to this cold and heartless void.

For weeks I've felt them slip away; for weeks I've felt a nameless fear, a line of dark and chilly water, rising from the depths inside of me. I've panicked often at the process, as it hit my guts, my heart, my throat, my ears. The friends I loved receded into unkept promises and empty words; they had no energy left over for my pain.

Somewhere in this process, I became abandoned. Somewhere in the journey out of childhood, I stopped feeling loved. My parents had done everything for me; they loved me deeply, but they never showed me how to love myself. They taught me how to brush my teeth and comb my hair, how to talk and think, how to make a bed and cook a meal, how to climb a cliff and drive a car.

But they never showed me how to love myself. Perhaps they didn't really know; perhaps it was a gift they didn't have to give.

I don't know how to love myself.

I'd never have known that if JF and Joyce hadn't retreated into coupledom. Now the feeling's fresh for me, that childhood shift from total love to separation. I've been shut out again, and it hits me in the same uncomprehending place it must have hit the three-year-old I was so long ago.

I'm alone! I've been abandoned...

Breathe.

What does it matter? Explanations, theories: they're dusty boxes piled in a vast attic. What can I do but shuffle them around? Who's to blame? Who's at fault? There's so much dead space in this attic, so much time surrendered to the past and future and what should be and what should have been...

I can't find the stairs; I can't get down into my body...

Breathe.

I'm a stranger to myself again; I can't find the keys to my own body; all the codes have changed; no one on the outside seems to have a clue how to support me. When any one tries, bless their souls, I only feel despair. Nothing fits or harmonizes; nothing feels safe. I want to scream and cry my way out of this, but I'm paralyzed. There's a weight on my chest, and emotion won't move. So many dusty boxes, pressing down on me...

Breathing in, I feel my stuckness.

Breathing out, I feel despair.

Now that's become a familiar pattern...

Can I live with that, instead of trying to change it? Maybe stuckness and despair are keys.

The answer has to be in what is happening. That's always how it works. Face what's in front of you. Align with your experience.

Can I surrender to despair and pain? I've given them so much power over me, made them so dark and evil. What if I embrace them?

NO!! I'll fail! I'll give up and die...

I'll lose my pride and separation, my control, my transcendence...

OK. I see that's bullshit.

I'll embrace the pain.

Breathing in, I welcome my pain. Good morning, pain, my friend; how are you today?

I hurt so much! There is a grieving that I can't release. Centuries of pain and hurt are flowing into it. Bottomless, centerless, endless: a black hole of despair.

Breathing in, I welcome my despair.

I can't do this! I can't surrender to despair. I'll lose everything I've worked so hard for...

Let it go. Working is a dream; it only feeds the ego...

I'm stuck in ego, then; I've got to --

Breathing in, I feel my ego. I feel the terror and the fear. My ego's only trying to protect and guard me. It only wants me to be safe; it's trying to be parent to the frightened little child...

Today we must go in to the despair. That is where the keys are.

Breathing in, I welcome all my children: fear, despair, surrender, pain, protection, anger, grieving, guilt...

Don't get mental.

There's an iron band across my guts. I want to feel.

What is it protecting?

Do not fill yourself with other people's energies. Your body's still in process. Honor your unique vibration.

I don't want to be alone.

You're not alone. Don't look into projected images for life. Find the heart of yourself, unique in all the universe.

Breathing in, I feel the tightness everywhere, descending on me like a chilly winter evening. I am alone. When I honor God, I lose the company of others. God makes me alone, brings me into the cave of aloneness. Where are my companions? Where is my support? How can I trust this when it brings me no love?

You know nothing of love except fairy-tale stories. Love is everything and everywhere. Until you feel it always, like the air you breathe, you don't have a clue what real love is.

Show me love. Now.

Love is you breathing here, writing these words, with tears dripping onto the paper.

That's sentiment. I want to feel the whole, unvarnished truth.

Darkness and despair are just as much a part of love as wedding bells and joy. Pain and ugliness and evil aren't separate from God. Love embraces everything, and finds it beautiful.

Then why am I holding myself apart?

You have refused to find love in your loneliness and pain, and so you must enter that darkness, to touch and know it intimately, to transform your fears and prejudices.

I'm afraid that darkness takes me farther from you.

Find me in the darkness. Seek me everywhere. Embrace me; ravage me. I am all creation. Nothing is, that is not Me.

My guts are tingling. Something's lifting.

Your ignorance is lightening. Come dance with me...

* * *

Monday, midnight

Tonight the full moon called me outside to indulge in wonder. I caught it rising over the hill, aligned directly opposite the setting sun. One side of the sky was gold; the other, silver. As the planet turned so clearly on its axis, strung between those two celestial poles, I went out spinning, for a walk.

Nature was radiant; the fingers of the trees burned with a golden glow, while shadows slowly thickened down below. The moon climbed higher as I walked into the forest. For maybe half an hour, as my eyes adjusted, all I saw was the advancing darkness. Finally my patience was rewarded, and the treetops opened up to let the moonlight in. Waterfalls of silver slid down tree trunks to the ground. The elves and fairies came out dancing; distant laughter tinkled on the wind.

"Do you believe in magic?" someone asked me earlier this week.

"I have to," I replied. "I'm living in the middle of it."

"Then why don't you have everything you want?"

"Because it's magic, not mechanics. Magic, by its very nature, isn't solid and predictable. Sometimes you have to let your eyes adjust so you can see it. Sometimes you have to surrender; sometimes you have to take charge. If you always got the same reaction every time you did something, it would be science, not magic."

"Oh."

THE GIFT OF RELATIVITY

I took another leap of faith after that. I decided that my healing process was more valuable than anything else I could do. Although I had no money saved, and rent was due, I stopped working.

Every day I danced out on the rainbow bridge, running through my feelings, dissolving fears, reaching out for help. "Since healing is my work right now," I told myself over and over, "I believe I should be paid for it. I'm doing an excellent job, and I expect to be supported."

Life cooperated. I got an invitation to move somewhere else, with new friends who'd been taking classes with me. I gave my notice at the cottage in the woods, and asked to use the security deposit for last month's rent. Despite the lease I'd signed, the landlord agreed.

Everything was moving fast. I often lost my balance, but I always got it back. Recovery time from shock or failure, once measured in months, was now down to days and sometimes even hours. I was taking on the biggest challenges I'd ever faced, in housing and income and health, and I was succeeding.

When Joyce and JF threw a housewarming party for themselves, I decided to go. Who knew what I might learn?

I learned, to my disappointment, that I still hurt.

It wasn't easy being with them in a crowd. Such a couple they'd become! I slipped away and went down to the creek where, in another age, Joyce and I had gathered rosebuds.

I headed for a quiet spot I loved. A canopy of trees arched over the water there, making a cool nest of shade from summer heat. For several minutes I leaned against a trunk and listened to the creek splash over rocks. My mind spun relentlessly. My heart felt as hard as a rock. It was as though a thousand cogs and gears were spinning wildly, but none of them engaged. The engine raced, but I couldn't get it into gear.

I forced myself to breathe into the pain and stuckness. "Breathing in, I feel my anger," I repeated over and over. Something moved inside of me. "Breathing out, I let my anger go." The anger swelled and disappeared, replaced by fear.

"Breathing in, I honor my fear; breathing out, I let it go."

As each emotion surfaced and receded, another took its place. In time, I moved on from emotions to relationships. "Breathing in, I honor my relationship with Joyce; breathing out, I let her go."

I found myself remembering people from my past, old lovers, friends I'd lost track of, all the way back to grade school, and childhood. Each breath carried me farther. Sometimes a new emotion would surface as I recalled a particular person; I kept breathing through them all.

After a while, I slid down to the ground, and stared across the creek at a cluster of leaves which were radiant with sun. As I breathed through my litany of feelings and friends, little by little, a breeze began to stir. The leaves shimmered, and I felt a lightness in my chest.

Through the branches I could see the party going on. Many of the guests had come outside to enjoy the afternoon sun. They strolled around the garden, or lounged on the deck; a small group played frisbee on the lawn.

I knew almost everyone here. I knew their personal histories, their moods and what they liked to talk about. As I watched, and breathed, I realized that I was not the only one having a hard time. Jason was scowling by the barbecue pit; Julie and Chris were huddled on the porch steps, doubtless going over the details of her recent divorce. Robert and Jon walked up the driveway, gesturing madly about some business deal. A few kids, squealing with delight, ran in circles around the oak tree.

Everyone was living in their own reality. Even though we occupied the same space and time, even though we shared a common goal in being here, no two of us were in the same experience.

Half-hypnotized, hyperventilating, I fell into a trance. My vision flattened out, and something opened deep inside of me.

Floating in front of the trees, hovering over the creek, I saw a giant, spinning sphere. It was magical, changeable, in constant motion. Arranged around it, in infinite variety, were trillions of dots. Each point in space gave access to a single point of view. The central event, that spinning ball of magic, could be seen from any of these vantage points. From each perspective, the event revealed another face, another truth, a different reality.

When I was not attached to any one perspective, I was free to move into a multi-dimensional maze of astonishing beauty and radiance. The instant that I chose a single feeling, or became judgmental, all the magic faded. Once I latched onto an attitude, and got caught up in justifying it, I was miserable. "Why insist I know what's right?" I asked myself. "Whatever I judge, I don't get to enjoy..."

And so I made my way back to the party, celebrating Joyce and JF's home, and their happiness together. I honored my own fear and sadness, and made a game of noticing how everyone had chosen a different experience of the same event.

At last I didn't have to decide who was right! I didn't have to waste precious energy defending my position, or backing myself into corners. As long as I allowed myself to move and breathe and change positions freely, anything was possible.

I remembered when Leilani had enlightened me about *haoles*, those who didn't breathe and couldn't change. "The nature of life is to move," she'd said. "Only the dead cease to change."

I heard a rustling in the trees. A breeze was coming down the creek. Sunlight sparkled through the leaves like diamonds.

I remembered the diamond Kim had given me. Everything is just a facet of the bigger whole; all of my experiences come from me, from my perspectives, my emotions, my beliefs. I pick and choose what will be my reality. Nothing is outside of me.

I swallowed air. The wind picked up. All around me, the trees tossed their manes like wild horses, in perfect rhythm with my breathing. When I held my breath, the wind abruptly stopped.

*   *   *

Saturday night

There's nothing outside of me. No love, no money, no power, no wisdom, no parents, no help or support.

Once I stop looking for these things outside myself, I can find them. They're inside of me.

And because I find them inside myself, I don't have to fight for them. Or work, or struggle, or compromise, or manipulate. No one else can keep them from me, ever. No one else can take them away. No one else has any power over them at all.

I feel this in my body now, in my heart, as well as in my mind. It's become reality for me. And it's moving me past fear.

The world will mirror back exactly what I choose to give myself. No more, no less. No one else has anything to say about this. Other people may be the avenue through which I receive what I want, but they are not the source. I am.

This is why there is no justice in the world, why the "good" may suffer while the "bad" may win. It has nothing to do with deserving. We get what we give ourselves, not what we earn.

When we believe we have to earn something, we give our power away. Someone else will gladly pick that power up, and use it for themselves. They'll make us dance through hoops to "earn" what was ours from the start.

I'm no longer interested in "earning" anything. I'm willing to work for myself. I'm willing to love myself, unconditionally, and not work at all.

I'm willing to give myself the world.

- $ -

COCREATION

Wednesday

I've moved myself out of the woods, and back into the bigger world. The living room of my new home has vaulted ceilings and a great stone fireplace, and space enough to hold a class of twenty people. No more working psychic fairs and coffee shops!

My bedroom overlooks the valley. From my window, I can see the forest where I used to live, in the writing hideaway I'd dreamed about. I can write in this huge house; I don't need to hide away.

I'm learning I don't have to do this all alone. Karen and Jenean are renting this new house with me; by pooling our resources, we can all come out ahead.

None of us have solid paychecks. Karen's massage practice ebbs and flows from one week to the next. Jenean's business at the coffee shop is relatively steady, but when a toilet backs up or the freezer blows, she can lose a hefty chunk of change.

They both seem willing to accept whatever comes, financially. There is no guilt, no blame. We pool whatever cash we have, and together we decide on our priorities. Far from kicking in my fears, they are teaching me not to worry at all about money. Jenean, especially, has an attitude that it will all work out. And over and over, it does. Not always as I might expect, or want, but it does all work out.

I am letting money worries go. It's like learning to float in the ocean: the more you relax, the lighter you get. Waves may come and knock you off balance, but if you just relax, you'll soon float back up to the surface. If you struggle and fret, the water can't support you.

Living here, with both of them, I'm learning to accept
whatever comes, without attaching a lot of excess emotion to it.
A bill is just a bill; a financial agreement is only business. When
I add fear and shame and guilt, I weigh myself down. Why stuff
my swimming suit with rocks now that I'm learning how to float?

*   *   *

One evening, shortly after we'd moved in, I held my first class at the new house. A group of fifteen came. While rain dripped off the rhododendron leaves, we sprawled around the great stone fireplace, and talked about "Unconditional Relationship."

"Most of the time, when we believe we're giving," I said, "what we're really doing is investing. A gift is freely given, with no strings or expectations. An investment wants a payback.

"We'd never dream of lending or borrowing money without a clear contract detailing terms. Neither would we walk into a store, start working, and then expect someone who had never hired us to write out a paycheck at the end of the day.

"Yet we do that all the time in our relationships. We just assume that if we give, if I take care of you, you must take care of me. When we discover that the other person hasn't made the same assumptions, we get pissed.

"Sometimes we get into the habit of giving generally, to everyone, to no one in particular. Giving becomes a part of our identity. We try to be thoughtful, or generous, or 'nice'. When I am feeling powerless, I try to create a certain obligation on the part of others, and of life. I do unto others as I would have them do unto me. Not out of love, but out of fear.

"Shrewdly, desperately, I try to store up brownie points against some future need. This strategy is how a lot of people think of karma."

"But isn't that how karma works?" a young man asked.

"I don't think so anymore," I replied. "Everything is moving faster now. I believe the good I do today returns to me today; so does the bad. Instant karma. If I want to receive support at some future time, then all I have to do is ask, and open up to the support I need in that moment. What I did ten years ago won't matter anymore. No one's keeping score except the victims."

Someone coughed. Bodies shifted; papers rustled. This was a sore spot, I could tell. No one wanted to face it head on.

"Let's try an exercise," I suggested. "Everybody move onto the floor into a circle." There was a scramble for positions.

"Now turn sideways, to the right, so that you're facing someone's back." A stationary conga line materialized, looping back on itself.

"Give the person in front of you a shoulder rub." Hands got to work. I waited a few minutes.

"Is everybody having fun?" I asked.

After a pause, Jenean volunteered, "This is kinda hard. I get confused with two different people's energies at once. And if I try to dig in with my hands, my shoulders can't relax."

"Me, too," someone else piped in.

"Try harder," I demanded.

A few more minutes passed. Tension mounted.

Finally Scott stopped. "Time out. I can't do it. My muscles can work, or relax, but not both."

"Yeah," Sharon declared. "I can give a great massage, or I can get one. Just not at the same time."

"Okay, let's stop," I said. "Thanks for playing along. Let's turn back toward the center of the circle." Backs stretched, fingers cracked.

"Remember, when you're struggling, how the body breathes," I said. "First in, then out, then in again. Each direction has its turn.

"When we're stuck in automatic giving mode, like robots, we can't relax enough to receive. Receiving is an art that all too few of us have mastered."

A sudden burst of rain drummed on the roof.

"There was a time," I shared, "not so many years ago, when I was fiercely determined to be independent. I put up a proud front, hid my feelings and my troubles, and refused all offers of help.

"I clung to the delusion that I was making it on my own, but in my heart I knew that wasn't true. In my heart, I didn't feel that I deserved anything: love, support, a car, a decent job.

"I couldn't possibly accept what anyone wanted to give. This had nothing to do with them; it was my own sense of unworthiness, my own self-punishment for failing. Stubborn pride slammed half the doors to my salvation; and foolish judgment locked the rest. Soon enough, I was trapped in a prison of my own making."

We did another exercise, to practice opening our hearts, and coming out of our own private jail cells. One way to open the doors is to ask for what we want, right here and now.

We went around the circle, stating what we wanted to create for ourselves this evening.

Maiya, who was first, started with a long sigh. "What I'd really like is coziness and comfort. When I go this deep, I like to feel more connected."

After some quick negotiating, we all scooted together, on our knees, into a giant group hug. We practiced staying with it for awhile, breathing together, letting all the love in, like a litter of puppies or kittens sprawled across each other, totally content, soaking it up.

The candles flickered and the rain turned to a gentle drizzle. Someone said that Maiya's request had been a gift for them, too. Giving and receiving happened simultaneously, in the same event. As Maiya received what she had asked for, she created a gift for us all.

Karen took a breath. "Last week I made a birthday package for a friend who's far away. It was fun to smile and feel all the wonderful feelings as I put it together, and sent it off with love. It's funny how when you give away as much love as you possibly can... you are full again."

Scott added, "Each time I truly give, the gift enriches me. Each time I gratefully receive, I allow someone else to practice giving. It's a mutual benefit. When I'm coming from my heart, the gift is complete in itself. It happens in the moment, and it's done. Nothing hangs on, waiting for fulfillment down the road."

"That's right," I said. "Live life in the moment. In the moment, we have all we need, if we can only open to receive it. I'm so glad I had the courage to unlock my prison cell. Why, now that I'm out here, I've gotten to meet all of you."

I looked around the circle at a sea of smiles. It was true: a few short months ago I'd been in hell, abandoned and alone. And now I was being supported, on many levels, by a whole new circle of friends.

"I can't remember how I ever managed to believe that I was independent. Everything about me, on every level -- down to the food I eat each day, the chemicals which form my bones, the thoughts I hold, the money in my wallet, the love I constantly receive, the very air I breathe -- all of this has come from somewhere else. It's borrowed from life, or given to me as a gift. I've created none of it. I take it in and use it, but I don't know how to make it on my own.

"It's a miracle that I am here. It's a blessing beyond anything that I deserve, or I could ever earn, to just be born here in this world, with eyes and ears, with feelings and a heart. If I believe that I can earn my keep here, I am daft. There's nothing I can do, or give, to match the value of what I've been given.

"And so, I must be humble. All I can do is receive these gifts graciously, share what I've been given, pass it on gladly. We're all part of a vast, immeasurable cycle. Everything we own, and everything we are, is borrowed.

"When we ask for what we truly want, and let it in, the world moves into alignment, and everyone around us is blessed. We pass beyond investments and earning; we even pass beyond giving and receiving. There is only openness, and willingness, and acceptance, and flow. We step into the flow of life ongoing; we pass into the realm of Unconditional Relationship.

"And this is where I'd like to leave off talking now. I thank you for your many contributions to my life."

There were a dozen thank-you's from the room, and then a great, magical silence. In that silence, as the rain dripped from the leaves, we drank our fill.

* * *

That night I had a dream. Life, or God, or the Creator --
whatever word you want to use; from every perspective the same
great force took on a different face -- was playing a game with
me. We were weaving a great tapestry, made up of countless
interlocking lives in every direction. The immense, unfinished
fabric stretched across a dozen galaxies.

I would offer up a thread: a feeling, a goal, an unresolved
issue. The weaver would hold it up against the greater tapestry,
turning it this way and that, squinting, checking for color and
texture, deciding where it might best fit. As he turned, his face
became a woman's, or a golden shadow, or a song.

Often he would keep one of my threads, and add it to the
ongoing picture. Sometimes she would gently shake her head, and
hand it back to me. "Not yet," the light would say. "A bit more
green is needed first, and then a splash of anger, and over here a
triumph and a tragedy."

I'd take the thread back, and return it to my pile. Even
when a cherished dream was handed back unrealized, I didn't feel
rejected. "It's not time," I told myself. "We've got all of the time
in the world."

"That's right," the weaver smiled at me. "In time, every
dream will come true. This particular thread needs a companion
over here, someone you must meet first, an idea you have not yet
heard, a couple feelings you have not quite mastered. Hold it in
your heart; we'll come back to it later."

I did so with relief. Who knew more than life itself, with
its great overview and patience? Not every possibility is right or
ripe for manifesting every moment. All things have their season.

When it's time for a particular dream to be born, life
offers no resistance; everything falls into place. We meet the right
people, hear the right messages, at last receive the invitation, get
the tickets, lose the old job, make the sale. All without effort.

When we work in harmony with life, everything becomes
easy, effortless, and enjoyable. When we resist, and keep pushing
an untimely dream, our life collapses into struggle, pain and
separation.

Sometimes, life agrees to support a particular dream, and

we refuse to believe that it's possible. We must surrender our fears and our sense of undeservingness if we really want to work in harmony with life. All things are possible with God.

As I rummaged through my threads, I started humming. Life joined in. She encouraged me to look past the obvious threads, the superficial fantasies, to go deeper and deeper within, finding threads, making threads, spinning my own. One by one I held them up.

"This?"

"No."

"This?"

"Close. Have you got one just a little longer?"

"Let me tie these two together."

And so we played, singing and working, each intent on our separate tasks. I remembered our class from the evening before, when Maiya asked for what she wanted and created blessings for us all, when giving and receiving became one.

"Is that what you are doing?" I asked life. I knew that he could share my thoughts.

She smiled and took the thread I offered. "I've been waiting for that one." He shook it out and deftly wove it through the cloth. "Watch."

A shooting star blazed through the sky, with my thread as its tail.

"Sometimes I wait a long, long time," she whispered. Her face dissolved into a mist, illuminated from within, a glowing Milky Way, twinkling and fading. "Without your threads, I cannot weave the tapestry. Without the weaver, all your threads lie useless on the ground."

"So you're saying we are partners?"

"Absolutely. That's why I created you."

"You create the galaxies. Why do you need me?"

"You're my link into the human world, my hands and fingers in the human dream."

"Why me?"

He laughed, and for a moment his fingers stopped weaving.

"Not only you. Every being in creation is participating in

this great, ongoing universe. Together we are making all this up."
Suddenly it dawned on me. "Every day's the First Day."
She smiled at me, radiantly. "Exactly. Every moment is the First, the Only, the Original. It's never done, it's never just beginning. We're in the middle of creation. We can make it any way you like."

"All of us together."

"Yes."

"Any way we like."

"That's right."

I stood up on my tiptoes. "I'd like to see the tapestry from your perspective, please."

She took my hand and pulled me. "Breathe," he said, in a deep voice. "Relax." They stretched me in every direction. My feet stayed on the ground, in David's shoes, and the rest of me elasticized like taffy.

My threads lay far below me, on the ground. All my feelings, my thoughts, my ambitions and dreams, my losses and my loves were gathered loosely like a nest around my feet.

I looked up. Stars swam through my body. Gods smiled in every direction.

There was nothing to do but enjoy. The awesome unfolding of all God's dreams, through us and in us and as us, bloomed in every corner of the universe.

I saw that everything is, and always was, and always will be, absolute perfection. Nothing is finished, yet nothing's left undone. I could appreciate the beauty of each thread, each life, the love that's shining in each dream we've given to the whole. I came to see that God was dreaming in us, and through us.

All God does is dream creation into being.

Creation is the key. Until we consciously join in that process, God will only be a distant presence, and we mere victims at the hand of fate.

"So this is how it's done," I said. "Once I move into the miracle of cocreation, we're all one. Everything is possible. We're doing this together."

The universe turned toward me. An infinity of beings

looked up from their work on the tapestry, sewing together eternity and time, passing the shuttle back and forth to God; and each of them was smiling in acknowledgement.

"I'm ready to go back," I whispered.

And I did.

DAILY LIFE IS NOT AN INTERRUPTION

Weeks went by. I came out of my shell, playing and laughing and creating money by the fistful. Visitors dropped from the sky; my classes grew; the consulting business flourished. All I ever did was share what I was learning, and that seemed to be enough.

I journaled on an almost daily basis, trying to record the miracles as they unfolded. My book about the Bungalows was a project from the distant past, gathering dust in a corner of the closet. I'd given up on getting rich, and had settled instead for living in the daily flow.

Then one morning Barbara, my friend of twenty years, invited me to drive out to the desert past the Cascade Mountains. The kids in her private school, StarChild Learning Center, were due for a camping trip. She wanted to scout out a campground.

We rendezvoused outside the gym where she'd gone for her morning swim. She was waiting in the StarChild van, her thick gray hair still wet.

"David, my friend," she greeted me with a hug. "It's been a long, long time. What's happening in your world?"

"Everything and nothing," I replied, mischievously. "I'm making money doing what I love. I never have to dread getting up in the morning to go to a job I've outgrown. I don't even have to go to a job: people come to me. I sit in my beautiful house, and they bring money to me. I work my own schedule, take off when I please, answer to no one.

"Other than that, not much. And you?"

"Don't be a shit. I'm happy for you. Now could you wipe that Cheshire Cat grin off your face?" Rummaging through a bag, she asked, "You want an apple or a bagel?"

"Plain?" I asked. "No cream cheese or jelly?"

She nodded.

"Apple, please. You want to share?"

As we drove, we caught up with each other's lives. It's amazing how much can go on in just a few months! She was working with a group of parents to incorporate the school as a non-profit. There were always new stories about the kids. We gossiped about mutual friends, and shared what we'd been learning.

And so we passed the time away, climbing out of the green Willamette Valley, through the mountain passes, and into the high desert. Beside us, through the thinning trees, a stream kept pace with the road. Water sparkled in the early autumn sunlight.

"I don't see anything that looks remotely like a camp-ground," Barbara said, handing me a map from under her seat.

"But we're in the right spot," I answered her unspoken question. "Not that I would want to bring a couple dozen kids out to a desert for the weekend."

"How much farther?"

"Less than ten miles, straight ahead."

Only scrub brush lined the road. The mountains ringed a vast plateau, so flat you could see cars and houses miles away, the dust plumes rising from the plain. The sun was so intense and clear, it showed up streams and valleys on Mt. Jefferson, some sixty miles in the distance.

She shrugged and kept on driving.

"Strange came to visit me a couple weeks ago," I said.

"Strange de Jim from California?"

"The merry manifester himself, with a new manuscript in tow, called *Billions of Virgins Near Ecstasy*. He claims it's a true story, with triple-jointed mininuko courtesans and the odd temple masseuse, not to mention the Olympic gymnast with the amusing sexual problem. He's quite the storyteller."

"You sound sad."

"Oh, it just brought up a lot of stuff for me. You know: my own book, which even as we speak is rotting on a shelf, unfinished."

"Why don't you finish it?"

"That's what JF always asks me. 'How's the book coming along?' Every time he calls, I feel guilty.

"Despite all the miracles I'm creating, I'm still not unconditionally rich. I'm doing what I please, and paying all of my expenses, nothing more."

"But you're still writing?"

"Almost every day. The only problem is, I'm not writing about money. I write about classes, and dreams, and friends, and emotional processes. But I don't write about money."

"Too much daily life gets in the way, eh?"

"That's how it feels. Besides, I'm not in a position to lecture anyone about big bucks. I had my chance, and I blew it. Until I make a bundle, I kind of feel I'm not the expert to be telling other people how to get rich."

"You have to be rich to have something of value to share about money?"

"It would help. You know, give me credibility."

"You and your credibility! It doesn't all happen at once, you know. The big things change in tiny baby steps. You've worked with toddlers before. Remember?"

I nodded yes. I had worked with Barbara, at StarChild, back in the days of my low-paying, emotionally-rewarding jobs. Around the time that I spun off the roller-coaster tracks entirely.

"Learning to walk takes patience and excitement," she continued. Once she started on a subject, she rarely let it go. "It also takes a certain level of development and motor skill. You can't walk till your body's ready. Most of all, though, it's a lot of falling down and getting up again. You always want to go from A to Z without a break, my Aquarian friend. You always want to skip the baby steps."

"Well, I'm not skipping them any more. Like it or not, I'm sure taking my time. First I got the concepts down, and then I worked through the emotional resistance and fears. Now I'm moving back into my body. I'm already starting to sense the physical ways that money can flow, like blood through the veins, like electrical activity along the nervous system..."

Barbara slammed on the brakes. In front of us, the road

dropped down, abruptly, into an enormous chasm.

A geological wonderland opened up in the earth, a wonderland that had been totally invisible a minute before. Five hundred feet below us, the Deschutes River wound through raw rock palisades. Down in that canyon were terraces, two lakes, an island, a marina, five separate campgrounds with hundreds of manicured campsites, trees and lawns fed by sprinkler systems, and a sheltered children's beach. We'd struck gold.

At the bottom of the canyon, we stopped and got out of the van. As we dipped our toes into the lake, Barbara asked why I still reacted to money in a black-and-white, either-or way.

"You seem to believe you can write, *or* make money; you can sit down alone at your desk, *or* see clients. Why is it so hard to integrate both? I put on a dozen different hats every day, Mom and Teacher and School Director and Counselor and Cook and Playmate and Friend. I've seen you do that kind of synergistic juggling, many times before."

"This is different. When I focus on the book, I can't seem to do anything else. I go too deep; it takes me too long to get into that state," I complained.

"You want it to be perfect," she accused me.

"I don't know how to do it any other way," I answered. "It's too big; I have to concentrate too much. There's too many parts to hold together at once. I get angry when my flow is always interrupted."

"Don't make it so hard. What if you stopped thinking about daily life as an interruption? When I'm truly in the flow, everything contributes to the process; everything's a gift. There are no 'interruptions'."

"I know you're right, but I can't seem to apply it here."

"You've taught yourself that ordinary life is somehow different and separate from what you're trying to write about."

I caught my breath and gulped. I must have turned my body away, too, because the next thing she did was laugh.

"Don't you try to turn away from me, David Cates. Get back over here and face this."

I cringed. "You mean ordinary life is trying to get back

into my book?"

"Yes."

"And I keep calling it an 'interruption'."

"You got it."

By now I was thoroughly humiliated. "So life has been supporting me all along, and I kept pushing it away. I was trying to stay pure and clear, so this book would be pure and clear, and people wouldn't pick up my misunderstandings and bad habits."

"Perfectionism is one of your worst habits," Barbara reminded me, a bit too cheerily.

"I keep talking about integrating all of life with money, and here I go separating them again."

"It's not really *again*, dear heart. You just haven't gotten this deep into it before. This is a new level, and on this level, for you, they've always been separate. Don't be too hard on yourself."

I splashed a bit in the lake, and a stream of thoughts poured through me.

At first, this book had been a simple memoir, based upon my conversations at the Bungalows. That was straightforward enough: I had my notes, my guest files, all the research. All I had to do was write them down.

Before I'd left the Bungalows, I had a pretty clear grasp of the principles the rich had shared with me. But in Oregon, something new began to happen. I got personally involved. My awareness was shifting in profound new ways, and I had to practice. I was learning how to walk again, and there was lots of falling down and getting up. This was slowing down my writing, but it helped me integrate the information, make it real.

Now I realized how this could become a book about real life, lived unconditionally. It could tell the truth about a spiritual journey into the heart of abundance.

All these daily details weren't interruptions; they were gifts; they were the very essence of the process. From JF to Jeckyl, from screaming fits to rosebud leis, life was helping me create.

I looked up at the canyon walls. The rock formations were

laid bare for all to see; every struggle and stress in the earth was mirrored in those jagged lines and ripples. From this distance, it was perfectly beautiful.

And if I bared myself, like these rock walls, and shared my daily writings, we would have the record of a transformation. This is how life breaks apart the desert to create a magical oasis.

Barbara booked her campsites, I let ordinary life back in, and we had a wonderful day in the wilderness. Exhausted and enriched, we drove back home.

* * *

The next time I talked with JF about the book, I heard what I'm sure he'd said a hundred times before: "But David, you don't have to be rich first. This book is how you'll make your money. Don't put the cart before the horse."

The fortune doesn't come first; it comes after. Love doesn't come first; it comes after. First comes vulnerability and openness and risk. When we create a space inside us for the energy to flow, it will.

And until we create that open space, the energy won't come.

Unconditional Money is not something which already exists in the world. It's being created right here and now, in this book, as we live it.

I'm passing you the threads I have discovered; you're weaving them into your heart. Together we are calling into life a new relationship with money. We know the separate threads: money, love, acceptance, power, cocreation. Now we're weaving them together.

When each of us, in our own way, begins to practice this, we will succeed. Like pebbles tossed into a pond, we will make ripples. We'll show others how to cocreate abundance.

Then the blueprint life is teaching me, one "daily interruption" at a time, will become reality. The money you have traded for this book will find its way to me; the information you have craved is in your hands. By aligning with our deepest dreams, and asking for support, we've all created blessings for each other, and the world.

This is the new secret of wealth, the secret we're creating now. We don't need to make money in the old, unbalanced ways; from here on out, we're birthing something new.

PLAYING WITH MONEY

After my visit with Barbara, I saw daily life in a whole new light. The hours in the day became more precious. Despite what she had said about my either/or approach to writing, I couldn't spend an hour with a client, and use that same hour to write. I had to make some choices.

My time was now more valuable, at least to me. One way to express that value was to raise my hourly rate.

Just to make it worth my while, to push my buttons and really move some energy, I decided I would double what I asked from each client. Up to now, I'd asked thirty dollars for an hour of my time. In this new phase, I would ask for sixty.

First I sweated. Then I went into fear. Was I pricing myself out of the market? Guilt cropped up. Many of my clients weren't wealthy; who was I to price myself beyond their reach?

There were a lot of emotions to breathe through, a lot of thoughts to volley back and forth. It amazes me today that I spent so much time debating just how valuable my time was.

*   *   *

Monday afternoon

The more I charge, the more I can attract the people that I want to work with. The more I charge, the less I'll be tempted to hold back. I've been growing astronomically, and my work reflects that. It's time to honor where I am today.

Money isn't the real issue here.

The real issue is power.

I've always been willing to negotiate money with any client, to set up payment plans, to barter or trade. I've never wanted money to get in the way of anyone's access to growth.

But money, or lack of money, isn't what's in the way of anyone's access to anything. There are always ways to work around lack of money. Get creative, come up with alternatives, make offers, ask for what you want.

The wealthy do this all the time: they wheel and deal, bargain and trade favors. Disempowerment is not an issue, and so neither is funding. They assume they deserve whatever they can get. If they don't get what they want, it's no reflection on them; it's just a deal that didn't work.

Most everybody needs to juggle finances at some points in their life. But temporary shortage is different than chronic poverty. "Being broke is not the same as being poor."

When I was poor, I always assumed that if I couldn't afford something, I didn't deserve to have it. If something was beyond my budget, I just walked away; I never went and said, "I really want to do this, and I haven't got the money. Can we negotiate a different exchange?"

From this side of the looking glass, I see it differently. From here, I see that if I really want something, it's my responsibility to find a way to make it happen.

And I also see, to my surprise, that most of the things I've wanted, but didn't get before, I wasn't really ready for. I would never have admitted that before.

To have gotten those things I wasn't ready for, I would have had to change myself too much. That was the price I didn't want to pay, and money was only a reflection of that deeper cost.

I wanted to be limited. My limitations felt familiar, like a worn and comfortable slipper. Even when it fell apart, or I outgrew it, I didn't want to let it go.

Poverty and disempowerment became essential aspects of my self-identity. When I maintained them, I knew my place in the world, and I knew who I was. I didn't have to face a dizzying array of choices. I defined myself by making the same choices over and over.

These days, I no longer have that luxury. I'm not familiar to myself. I've outgrown my limitations. I'm a process in the act of becoming, a storm without a center. A boy without a home.

I no longer know exactly who I am, or what my place is in the world. Sometimes that excites me, and sometimes it's terrifying. I'm out here making this all up, spinning dreams out of myself, like a spider leaping off a tree. Will these dreams I'm spinning hold me up? Or will I simply crash, deluded, to my death?

I want to make up something which has not existed before, and to do that I must put myself on the line. Every day. Every minute of every day.

As I spin myself from one dimension to another, I am finding people who are also out here spinning new realities. They're not back on the ground, discussing change or moaning about life. They're in the air, like me, making this up as they fly.

These are the people I want to be working and playing with. They are, for better or worse, empowering themselves to live their lives by their own rules. Now that I'm leaving limitation and familiarity behind, I want to play with them.

For too long I have held myself in poverty because I didn't want to betray or abandon the people I loved who were poor. I held myself in slavery so I could minister to other slaves. That way no one ever had to change.

That isn't going to work anymore.

Today, I empower myself to ask for what I want, to really feel that I deserve it, and to risk whatever changes come into my life because of this emancipation.

This is my Declaration of Independence from poverty. Today I'm lifting anchor, and setting sail toward a new world, a world of fun and play and unconditional abundance.

To mark this occasion, I'm doubling my rates.

* * *

That Wednesday morning, I wrote a letter to my regular clients, informing them that I was raising rates.

No one saw the letter. I hadn't mailed it yet.

But the phone rang all day long. By Wednesday evening,

I had five appointments set. Thursday, between sessions, I sat at the kitchen table with envelopes and letters, signing and stuffing and sealing. The phone kept ringing. Caught up in the frenzy of abundance and support, I squeezed in three more sessions that evening.

Thursday was the biggest money day I'd ever had doing this job made in heaven.

I'd decided to empower myself, to do exactly what I truly wanted, to confront and work through whatever emotions came up for me, and to take action in the physical world.

Just committing to that process unleashed massive quantities of energy. Some of that energy worked inside of me, and some reverberated out into the world. My commitment dropped like a stone into a quiet pool of water, splashing up a mess, and sending ripples out in every direction.

The magical part, for me, was that life responded before it rationally had cause to. The feedback started pouring in before I'd even finished or mailed out the letters. My intention alone created these results.

Life is learning to trust me. When I say I will do something, when I commit to follow a process all the way through to the end, I am as good as my word. Because we are developing a new relationship of mutual trust, life believes in me. There's no more sabotage or hidden tricks.

I'm clear, and when I align with that clarity, life backs me up. It's like having a good relationship with a bank; after a while, they extend you credit just on your good name, without asking for collateral or co-signers. "You have a new project you want us to support? Here's the cash you need, up front..."

I like doing business this way.

It's fun to play with money.

- $ -

GRADUATION

In the spring, some six months earlier, I'd started doing client sessions out of Jenean's coffee shop. Sometimes people would wander in for a latte or a sandwich, and see me reading cards for someone at the back table. If curiosity outweighed their fear, they might sit down with me. A lot of fifteen-minute quickies turned into regular clients, and a lot of them sent friends.

The shop is out near a business corridor which houses Nike, NEC, Intel, and several other multi-million dollar corporations. A few miles farther out, the fields are harvested by migrant laborers; but next to the airport, it's not unusual to see mobile phones and power ties.

My clientele expanded into these professional circles. When I moved the business to my home, referrals increased. As the months went by, word was passed up corporate ladders. I saw secretaries, sales people, district managers, vice presidents, and even an occasional top executive. They often referred me to other executives.

Three weeks ago, the CEO from a booming restaurant chain paid me a call. At work, his colleagues had shared tapes from earlier sessions, in which we'd focused on the business, with questions about office politics and product sales, job promotions and timing for market campaigns. He was intrigued by my perspective and advice. How could someone who obviously had no business training speak so clearly about complicated business matters?

I didn't beat around the bush. My dealings at the Bunga-lows had trained me to meet powerful people head-on, as absolute equals. We dug into the details of his personal and professional life, and laid it all out on the table.

The business had been started by his father, who still controlled the board; family dynamics were stifling forward motion. The corporation was in crisis, at a major turning point, and my client was the linchpin upon which changes hinged. I recommended he decide how far he was willing to go.

After he left the table, I didn't hear a word from him for weeks. Then, all at once, he was ready for another session. I squeezed him in the next morning.

When he arrived at my house, the tension in the air was palpable. I escorted him through the big room where we held our classes, and into the dining nook where I did private consultations. The small talk lasted all of two minutes, and then he got to the point.

"Last time I was here, I told you that my parents and I have been battling for control of the company. They're old and tired and ready to retire, but they won't let go. Well, it's gotten worse. This week my dad called to announce that he'd retained a lawyer, and he suggested that I do the same. The war is on.

"I see the world I came from," he told me, holding out his left hand. "Cut-throat, competitive, paranoid. That's how my parents see life. Now they think their son has turned on them!"

He shook his head with disgust. "I'm tired of living in that world. I see another way of life," he looked toward his outstretched right hand. "A world based on harmony, cooperation, mutual support. Win-win.

"I know the words," he looked across the black-tile tabletop at me. "I don't know how to get there. Help me."

My heart melted open.

We talked for over two hours that morning, man to man, without the cards or jargon. I shared how I'd integrated my own life, found peace and flow and satisfaction. For every sticking point he stumbled on, I suggested a solution he might try. We created a relationship of trust and mutual respect; by my actions and example with him at that table, I showed him that it could be done.

Time stood still. The sunlight edged across the floor and disappeared. I felt like I was talking with my closest friend in all the world.

We did hard work that morning; I nailed him, over and over again. I showed him how to shift his attitude, release the fears, come back into alignment with his heart.

Whenever I went too fast, and he got defensive, we'd stop and breathe together. I'd remind him that we both were on the same side, working toward the same goal. I led him through a lot of dangerous and unfamiliar territory, and he kept pace with me every step of the way.

Finally we got to the crux of the war with his parents. He recited a well-reasoned list of complaints, proving how wrong and unjust and old-fashioned they were. He would have been persuasive in a court of law, but this was not a court of law. This was a court of the heart. We were looking for peace, and permanent solutions.

"I want you to try something totally different." I cupped my hands as though I were making an offering. "I want you to go in to them and give them back the company. Hand it over to them, lock, stock and barrel."

"I've been on the edge of that," he angrily agreed. "If I resign and move on, they'll kill the company, but at least I won't get caught up in its death-throes."

I shook my head no. "That's not what I mean," I said softly. "I want you to hand it back to them and say, 'Here, this is your baby; you created it; it rightfully belongs to you. I'm grateful that you've brought it into being. This really isn't mine; it's yours. I'm only here to back you up. Let's work in harmony on this. Please let me help you raise this baby so it grows the way you've always dreamed.'"

We both sat back in silence.

Minutes ticked by. He got it. The power in that action registered; I could feel the shift inside his heart and guts. At that moment, love became a tool to him, useful and practical, and surrender became the only way to truly win.

His parents thought they wanted power; he and I knew that they really wanted peace. Once the weight of the company fell back on their shoulders, they'd be overwhelmed with the responsibility. They didn't want to work -- and here was the sticking point, the magic button; just push it to release what's stuck -- they didn't want to work, but they did want to be honored and respected for the work they had already done.

They were trying to save what they had built, before it disappeared into a future beyond their control. If he could drop his own pride long enough to honor their achievement, he could end up home free. Instead of having to wrestle the company away from them, he could empower them to fully own it, and of their own free will to pass it on to him, as a timely and appreciated gift, from one generation to the next.

That afternoon I got three separate calls from people I knew at that company. "What did you DO to him?" they all wanted to know.

One of his closest confidantes told me that he'd already met with his parents. Someone else said that he'd come in, whistling, as though the weight of the world had slid off his back. The third one simply thanked me.

I simply thanked him back.

∗   ∗   ∗

That same week I fielded yet another skeptical executive. He was from a larger company, and he had also been exposed to tapes of my sessions with his colleagues. These same colleagues had warned me that he might be calling. They also warned me that he wasn't happy with my interference.

The Vice President of Finances sat down at my table, crossed his arms, and glared at me. "I'm a born-again Christian, and I want to know what you've been doing to my workers and my friends. Exactly what do you get out of this? Besides the money, such as it is."

He spat a look at the tarot cards I was shuffling. "I consider those to be the devil's tools. So you can imagine where I think you get your celebrated information."

I picked up the deck, swung my arm away from the table, and dropped all seventy-eight cards on the floor. Then I crossed my arms, sat back, and said, "What exactly do you want to know?"

In fifteen minutes we were talking Jesus and the Bible, and in twenty he was spilling out his doubts and fears to me. I asked him if he had a personal relationship with God, and he said yes he did. I asked him if he ever drove a car. He looked at me askance, but said yes, of course.

"Did you ever read an instruction manual before you mastered driving?" I asked.

"Yes, I believe so."

"But now that you know how to drive, do you still hold that instruction manual in your left hand while you steer the car with your right?"

"Don't be absurd."

"That driving manual was aimed at new and unskilled motorists, wasn't it?" I pressed. "Hasn't your skill level, and your years of experience, made that instruction manual obsolete for you? You can drive automatically now, safely, and get everywhere you want to go."

"Enough already; what's your point?"

"The Bible is an instruction manual for developing a personal relationship with God. There's nothing wrong with it; it does its teaching admirably. But once you've learned the lesson, once you've got that living, breathing, in-the-moment connection with the Lord, doesn't reading an instruction manual seem slightly disrespectful? You have its Author on the phone!

"Wouldn't you be better served, and serve the Lord better, too, if you talked directly to Him? If He's alive for you, and whispering in your ear every day, why do you go back to old letters he wrote you a couple thousand years ago? His words to you today are what you need today!

"If He's living in your heart, just drive the car; don't stop to belabor a line in the instruction manual. God will let you know what your instructions are today..."

We talked on and on, and he gradually came to know me, and to know where I was coming from. We found common ground beyond the jargon of opposing ideologies, in the everyday experiences of the human heart.

At the end of ninety minutes, he said, "Now I see what you've been doing to my friends: giving them a place to come and talk their lives back into sense. I want to thank you for that. You've helped me today. Now, how can I help you?"

I sat there, stunned. I was always focused on my clients, who were generally absorbed in their own business. No one had ever asked me, in a session, how they could help me back.

I felt so moved it was hard to get the words out. "Help me get my work out to the world," I think I said.

"OK," he answered. "Right off the bat, I come from marketing, and I want you to know you've got a marketing problem. I was told you were a psychic and a card reader; you're neither. You're a teacher and a counselor. I couldn't recommend a psychic to any of my Christian friends, but I could recommend you. You're doing much the same thing as psychiatrists downtown with their black leather couches and their hundred-dollar, fifty-minute hours."

"But I don't have their credentials," I protested. I had wrestled with this problem before.

"Young man, you have positively impacted the lives of at least a dozen people whom I know and love. Those are your credentials. I am going to send people to you, other businessmen and women, from other companies. I will send my friends and their families. What more do you need for credentials?"

* * *

Wednesday

It's almost a week later, and I still haven't digested that one. Maybe I haven't even swallowed it. Here I am, in back-woods Oregon, making a living as a psychic and a fortuneteller, miles away from big bucks and glamour, oceans away from the bungalows.

I'm hacking out my finances with friends who are also straddling the poverty line, and now my lot is thrown in with another band of rich folk.

I do the work that's put in front of me, and hold fast to my dreams. Every time the pot gets stirred, the same situations rise to the top; every time the drink gets shaken, it soon clears.

I'm working with people who want to master more than one dimension. I'm healing the split between matter and spirit, head and heart, wealth and poverty. I'm working this out in my life, in my body, in my relationships.

And I am arriving. Everywhere I go, I am arriving. Success has nothing to do with environment, with place or other people. Success is what I create from my own focus and desire.

I want to do work I love, work that is as rich and rewarding as play. I want to play with people who are opening and growing, who are turned on by the tools we are discovering, the shifts we are making into new realities. I want to make money, easily and graciously. And I want my work to be profound.

All this is arriving; it comes to me by special delivery, no matter where I am hiding. In a coffee shop, reading cards at the back table in the corner. In the Bungalows. In my office in my home. In my heart. In my body. Everywhere I am, life keeps arriving, and play, and success.

It's not outside me anymore. It's reflected out there in the world, but I know that it's living in my heart. I gave the gift back to God a long time ago. I handed my life back to him, and said, "Here, this is yours; this is your baby; you created it; it rightfully belongs to you. I'm grateful that you've brought it into being. This really isn't mine; it's yours. I'm only here to back you up. Let's work in harmony on this. Please let me help you raise this baby so it grows the way you've always dreamed."

We've been partners ever since, through thick and thin, richer and poorer, better and worse. This works because we aren't focused on ourselves; we're focused on the partnership, the union, the baby: we're focused on what we're creating together.

We keep passing the gift back and forth, eager to share, willing to surrender, focused only on what's best for what we're bringing into life. This is the secret at the heart of every great healing, every great marriage: life and love flow when we get

ourselves out of the way.
Stay focused on the flow. Let the baby lead the way.

* * *

As the doors to the penthouse elevator opened, we were greeted by a swirling hurricane of jazz. A half-million-dollars' worth of musical equipment glittered underneath the ballroom chandeliers. My client led me through the studio, past a concert drum set, and into a sitting room overlooking downtown.

"I hope this is OK with you," he said apologetically. "We're mixing my new album, and this is pretty much where I live."

"Not a problem," I replied, whistling at the view. "I can do the session here."

We plopped down on the floor and began.

Three hours later, after we'd covered everything from his last European concert tour to groupies to his childhood to how to get a movie made outside of Hollywood, we stood up and hugged. He handed me a copy of a magazine.

"I scored an interview with the Dalai Lama," he said. "He was an incredible man: completely present, totally peaceful. But he's never had to deal with sex or drugs or money. I can relate much more to what you say; you know what it's like to live this life."

He asked if I had a publisher yet for this book. I said I'd met so many authors and agents who had volunteered to help in the past few months that I couldn't keep track of them; they seemed to be falling out of the sky.

He smiled and said, "Good. Your path has obviously worked for you; I'd like to see you get your story out." Then he asked me to come back whenever I was in town, or in the mood to listen in while they recorded.

A small crowd of musicians had been waiting for us to finish. Before I could get out the door, someone started wailing on a guitar, and someone else picked up the rhythm on a tambourine. In the flurry of excitement, I was passed a gorgeous African drum, and there I stood, frozen with shock, in the midst of a jam.

The tapes were rolling.

How could I begin to match these incredible musicians?

I forced myself to breathe, and softly joined in.

No one seemed to be concerned about my lack of expertise. I was there; this was happening; the only person standing in my way was me. Ever since the Bungalows, I'd said I wanted to be playing with the most creative people on the planet. This was as good a place as any to begin.

- $ -

REDEFINING SUCCESS

Every day the phone rang with a dozen people wanting time with me. Everyone I saw referred their friends. In no time at all, I was swamped with new clients.

As I got better, the sessions went deeper. People got in touch with deeper issues, harder problems. One week, six new clients brought up buried childhood traumas. I felt overwhelmed. It was never my intention to become that kind of counselor.

The job made in heaven, which I'd created out of nothing, started feeling like a job. Too much of anything, even ice cream, gets to be a sticky situation. Day in, day out, the demands on my time never stopped.

My roller-coaster threatened to run off its tracks again.

I became a victim of my own success.

*   *   *

Tuesday, 9:00 pm

I want to learn new ways to love myself.

For three weeks now, I've felt the urge to go past words, to disconnect from my responsibilities, to hibernate in my cocoon. I'm not sure what's going on; I'm only sure I trust it.

A week ago last Monday, I began to cancel my appointments. I stopped answering the phone, declined all invitations, refused to make plans. I let people get mad at me, and work it out by themselves.

I played with whoever showed up, and stayed in the moment, spontaneous. I had a lot of fun, and laughed, and lightened up considerably. I put myself back at the center of my universe, and gave up every debt and obligation. If no one owed me anything, then it was only fair that I owed nothing back.

Every morning I got out my imaginary scissors, and cut whatever psychic cords I felt connecting me to people or activities. I walled myself inside a black cocoon, so no one could find me. I unplugged the phone and turned off the TV. And then I played, and did precisely what I wanted. Life flowed, and magic reappeared.

A lot of fears came up. I felt them and released them. I'm not responsible for anyone else; I can enjoy my life, alone or not. When I am playful, life plays with me, and strangers pop out of aisles in the grocery store, to wink and laugh and share a private joke. Nothing's hard. Laughter breeds laughter; light breeds light.

For a week, I lost my clientele. No one called. My bookings dwindled down to nothing.

Instead of freaking out, I pulled some cash advances from my credit cards, paid the bills, and took myself to dinner. I declined the opportunity to panic. As I held to my resolve, life bent a little to support me.

This morning I woke up with all the bedroom windows open to the breeze. My body was still tingling with light from one of my dreams.

In this dream, a man was on a hill inside a gym. I was on the floor, with many other people, sweating and miserable. He tossed me ribbons of scotch tape, as though he were fishing; I tried to grab them, and pull myself up to his level. With each attempt, I would get closer, until finally I'd reached the ceiling of the gym, and was moving toward him, hand over hand, effortlessly floating above the sea of writhing bodies down below.

He encouraged me, smiling and beaming and holding his end of the tape. When I reached him, I collapsed into his arms. I felt the most amazing love, a blend of every love I've ever known: father, mother, brother, son, lover, sister, wife. He was an angel; he was everyone I've ever loved; he was myself. As I melted into his embrace, my body filled with light and peace. I smiled, and let the waves wash through my heart.

Somehow, by disconnecting from the people and routines of ordinary life, I'd found myself in heaven once again, and brought that sense of magic back to earth.

When I awoke, I lolled in the sun at the foot of my bed, glowing, dozing, dreaming. The house was empty. When my stomach started grumbling, I padded down to the kitchen. Usually I don't cook when I'm alone; I stand up at the kitchen counter and wolf down some cereal, or grab a piece of toast. Today I wanted to be different.

What would I do if I was in love? I asked myself. Throw routine out the window; be here in this moment, have some fun.

Instead of cereal, I set the table in the dining room, turned on some early-morning easy jazz, opened windows to the autumn air, and cooked myself a breakfast of french toast with all the trimmings. I reveled in sensations, and consciously kept choosing love. When my stomach was full, I got up and took my tea out to the garden. The leaves were tinged with color at the tips; late roses and chrysanthemums still bloomed beside the fence.

I moved slowly and sensuously. I tried to imagine how good I'd want myself to feel, how much I'd want me to enjoy the morning, if I was in love with myself.

All I wanted was simplicity. I was grateful for my senses: to be able to see, and smell, and walk about the yard. Look at that, I'd say; or, how different the air feels on my skin, do you notice that autumn is here? The slower I moved, the easier it was to slide into that easy intimacy and appreciation. Life is good, I thought. How lucky I am to enjoy it.

With no effort at all, I moved into the house and cleared the table. All I noticed was the sunlight glinting off the china, and the smells of cinnamon and tea still lingering above the stove. Washing the dishes was fun; I sang to myself as I splashed in the bubbles. I did some laundry, drifted from one room to another, watering plants, dusting. The love I felt made this seem easy, and enjoyable. I was content to be here with myself, happy to have such a beautiful place to be in...

When I am living in a world that's totally alive, each moment brings another opportunity for love. There isn't any part of my day when I'm not in relationship. I can talk to the silver-ware, thank my breakfast, say good morning to the sun; and they respond in kind! For years I thought this was a harmless eccen-tricity; now I believe that it's the most profound thing that I do.

If I relate to the things around me as mere objects and possessions, I dehumanize myself; I become just one more thing. When I am in relationship with my environment, I feel supported and prosperous and whole. I am willing to become a fool, in order to make room for magic in my life.

After breakfast, I plugged the phone back in. It rang all morning long. Next week is filling up. At least, the time I'm willing to devote to clients is filling up; there are many hours, sprinkled through each day, that I've reserved for play.

I wrote some checks, and sent out a new batch of bills. I played and worked and did precisely what I wanted.

And now, at the end of the day, I'm feeling moved to sit down at my desk and write. I want to catch this magical feeling, of lightness and courage and peace; it's spreading like a net around my day. Slowly, through some process I don't understand, all my fears are being gathered and dispersed. Slowly, as I focus on what brings me joy, the tedium vanishes.

No one else knows the rules or the timing that will work for me. Only I do, when I have the courage to believe in myself.

When I drop into myself, deeper than words, removed from the demands of relationship, I can find the ribbons, the trail of bread crumbs, my private passage to the future. Once I find the trail, then I can share it.

When I am lost, there's only one thing to be done: stop wandering, stop searching, go within.

*　　*　　*

In the middle of my hibernation time, I got a phone call from an old friend who was staying at an artist's colony in California. Over the years, Kenny's sent me postcards from around the country, as he's hopped from one paid writing internship to the next. Without him, I'd never have known that such things existed.

When Kenny called, I slipped out of my hibernation cave, and drove down the coast to visit him.

I fell in love with Saratoga. The colony was centered in a mansion in the hills near Santa Cruz, completely isolated on a huge estate, with gardens and trails and half a dozen guest cottages. Painters sketched among the trees. Musicians played in the great hall. Dancers somersaulted down the lawn.

The creative energy and camaraderie sparked a longing I had never felt before. Here were committed artists, totally engaged with their respective visions, being totally supported in the world. Here were Bungalows, not for consumers, but for creators and magicians. In my heart, this felt like home.

As I strolled around the grounds at Saratoga, and visited the artists' studios, I came to some decisions. I decided I was finished playing, for the time, with clients and personal growth. From here on out, I only wanted to create.

I had a chat with life again, my cocreative partner: *"Thank you very much for helping me create those jobs made in heaven. Thank you for supporting all those dreams. It was more than I'd imagined life could be. I'm ready to move on to other games. Would you still like to play?*

"I want to be an artist now; I want to focus on my writing. This place has been an inspiration for me. Now it's time to finish up the book."

* * *

Sunday morning

I've been releasing: letting go of the old, setting free the energy that's been locked up in the past. Every night I make a fire and I burn another stack of memories. Jenean and Karen join me from time to time. We sit in the great dark living room, with the deerskin drums on the wall, and the fire dancing off the vaulted ceiling. Sometimes we share a special memory before we toss another photograph or letter to the flames.

It started with Jenean. She stripped her bedroom walls and gave away the pictures and the painted clock, the flower baskets and the lacy hearts. Then she rummaged through her closet. Piles of clothes went out the door. Into the vacuum came a thunderclap of inspiration. For several nights now she's been up, burning with creative fever, painting power animals in a design that she saw in a dream.

Karen's room came next. Tonight she cleaned her desk out, and brought stacks of papers to the fire. File after file went up in flames; the heat was so intense we started shedding clothes. One by one she burned a special stash of love letters, from old relationships, which she had used to boost her self-esteem when she felt low on happiness, or far away from love. She's learned to love herself now. In the center of her bedroom mirror is a post-it note that says it simply: "Care for Karen".

I began with old drafts of this book, then moved on to business cards and flyers. Tonight I got the correspondence out, the cards and letters I'd collected as mementoes of relationships long gone. I blessed each person as I let them go, laughing and crying as I gave them over to the purifying flames.

I'm glad that I have learned new ways to release, to move old energy, to get myself unstuck. If I hadn't worked at this new process for the last few weeks, I'm sure I'd have created fever in my body, to burn this all away. Now I listen to my body: when it needs rest, I give it rest, and it stays healthy. When it needs exorcism, I release. We've learned to work in harmony.

I meditate on transformation as the fire turns the pages into heat and light and ashes. If I want to light up my life, the price to pay is living with the ashes.

Time flies. I'm ready to move on.

- $ -

WALKING ON A TRAIL OF STARS

Thursday, dinner-time

I've spent the whole day watching clouds. Autumn rolled in through the valley yesterday, a thick gray fog that slowly blotted out the distant hills, and then the pine trees in the valley. By this morning my car, parked on the street beside the house, had disappeared. By noon I'd forgotten my name.

As I watched through open windows, a gentle rain slid from the sky. I turned on the furnace, and huddled in a blanket over the vent in my bedroom. My writing sat beside me in piles on the floor. I couldn't take my eyes off of the sky.

Later in the afternoon, the clouds broke; now they're building up again, in time for sunset. Spots of color dot the fragile eggshell blue. A parade of flying-saucer clouds, round with swirling edges, hovers over town.

Down in the valley, and creeping up the hills, the trees glow with the burnished care of autumn. My eyes, knowing the colors cannot last, drink them in, determined to remember everything. I cannot say why this is so important. Perhaps I've realized that my dreams could spring to life at any moment, and carry me away. I might reach up and catch a ride on those clouds; it might be time to leave this magic hillside.

Last week, in one of my sessions, I had a vision of my client growing bigger and bigger, crossing mountains, stepping from one ocean to another, then striding off the globe itself and into empty space.

"You're walking on a trail of stars," I told her. "No, wait; that's not true. The stars aren't there already. There's nothing underneath your feet but empty space.

"Each time you put your foot down, a star sparks into being. Light marks that spot and holds you up. You're making your own path through the heavens, and leaving a trail of stars behind you as you go."
I have the feeling something similar is happening to me...

* * *

I threw down my bags on the high, old-fashioned bed. *Herman Melville Room*, said the sign on the door. His books were lined up on the mahogany dresser, beneath a stormy seascape. *Moby Dick, Billy Budd, Typee*. The bedside table had its own leather diary, filled with musings from previous guests. I could smell the salt air through the open window.

I was at the Sylvia Beach Hotel, a writer's paradise.

One of the owners, an amazing woman called Goodie, had warned me that a flock of cutting-edge thinkers was descending on the hotel after a week-long conference. She'd invited me to come down to the beach and join them.

I didn't spend much time unpacking; there was too much exploring to do. Each room at the hotel is dedicated to a different author, and decorated to reflect their times and tastes. The Ernest Hemingway Room sports trophy heads, mosquito netting and an old metal typewriter; Dr. Suess' Place is piled with toys beneath a zany mural of the Cat in the Hat.

In the first half-hour I met seven authors, a couple filmmakers, three educators, and a priest. We talked through Friday dinner, a leisurely four-course affair, about the future of the planet, brain research, spirituality, the state of publishing, mass migrations, and human evolution. I joined in as an equal, though my only credentials were personal experience.

Everyone listened.

I had a lot to say.

The evening slipped into night, blessed with an early moon skimming the waves. A few of us sat on the third floor balcony, off the cozy library, and carried on till well past midnight. The synergy of all those minds with all those different bits of information was exhilarating. I found myself, later on in my room, furiously writing notes for a new book. Suddenly my ideas didn't seem so off-the-wall: here was confirmation and encouragement from several different fields.

At breakfast I sat next to one of my heroes, Joseph Chilton Pearce. We talked about children and genetics and how to educate the computer generation. I shared about StarChild, and some ways to handle parent overload. He got excited about applying those methods to large audiences at workshops.

That afternoon I met with a filmmaker who'd documented Krishnamurti's last years. We talked about presence and spirituality, about how to maintain innocence while swimming with professional sharks.

On and on the conversations went. I'd landed in a brand new world, a writing world, and every one I met was a creator.

Goodie took the cake. She wasn't an artist like everyone else, but in creative power she matched anyone there. She had a most unusual medium: her creation was this gathering.

Over Sunday brunch, someone asked her how she came to start such a unique hotel. As usual, she had a story.

"When my kids hit adolescence, I wanted a life for myself again. But I'd been a Mom for so long, I couldn't really think what else to do. This perplexed me. Then one afternoon I got into the car and drove up towards Seattle on the interstate. I was looking for some inspiration.

"All of a sudden, I saw this field, and knew it was the one. I pulled the car over, crawled through the fence, and sat. I vowed I wouldn't move until I had a vision, and decided what to do next in my life. The nights were cold, so I knew I'd be motivated to make a decision before long.

"What I thought about is how I love creative people. Now, I'm not very creative myself. In fact, I often say I'm proof that even people without talent can succeed if they will only persevere." She was exaggerating, of course. She was always painting whimsical patterns on tables and walls, and had already published two books of quotes.

"So I thought to myself, How can I attract great thinkers

and creators? And how can I get them to hang around long enough to talk with me?

"All at once the answer came: a hotel on the beach. Everyone loves the ocean. And if they're staying overnight, or for the weekend, you've got plenty of time to talk.

"I crawled back through the fence, climbed back into my car, and went back home. It wasn't even dark. The next day I drove to every realtor on the Oregon coast, in the little sun belt from Florence to Lincoln City. I told each of them I wanted a hotel on the beach.

"Most of them laughed. One of them showed me a shabby old building in Newport, a transient flophouse. It needed lots of work, but it was right on the beach. I wrote a check for five thousand dollars deposit, and drove back home shaking. I had maybe fifteen dollars in my checking account. I spent the whole drive trying to figure out how I'd cover the check.

"I had a friend from grade school, Sally, who I called to ask for help. She not only loaned me the money, she got so excited by the concept that she joined in as a partner.

"We got all our friends to do the rooms for free. The deal was that you got to do one room, dedicated to any author you wanted, and furnished in their style. In return, every year you got free time at the hotel. All Sally and I had to do was the exterior. Our friends were ecstatic to have full creative freedom, to build shrines to their favorite authors, to be part of something fun and magical.

"And of course, they yacked to their friends all through the remodeling. We got tons of free publicity, from local news shows to the *New York Times*. From the day we opened the doors, we were booked up.

"And now I split my time between the coffeehouse in town, and the hotel on the beach. Thousands of people a year come through my life. I have all the fascinating conversations I could ever want. When authors do their book promotion tours, they all stop by for a break. Sometimes they come here to write.

"Without ever leaving home, the world comes to my door. I just open up and let them all in. I couldn't ask for a better life."

When the weekend finally ended, I was buzzing. I had to run on the beach for nearly half an hour to calm myself enough to sit still for the drive back home.

*   *   *

The end of time

My cage is being rattled -- hard. Some psychic hurricane or earthquake's been unleashed. I didn't even know that I was in a cage, but as it's shaking, I keep banging into walls and floors and ceilings. I'm being thrown against one limitation after another.

These limits are so deep they feel unconscious. A certain line of thought goes down, and suddenly, there's a boundary. One emotion follows another, like bricks laid into a wall. Somewhere overhead, habitual fear hardens into a ceiling, and every dream that doesn't fit into this comfort zone is out of sight and out of mind.

This rattling of the cage has cracked it open: not completely, but just enough to let in light and sound and smells from other places, from the larger world I left behind. I'm waking from a tight and healing dream; this life I have created here in Oregon was wrapped around me like a silvery cocoon.

And now it's splitting open.

Everything I've shared with you is true. These stories came from life. Of course, I chose the ones to tell, and strung them like so many beads along my own line of assumptions. I had a personal journey to make, a private path to follow. That path has teetered at the edge of our communal money map for almost three years now. Today it's falling off completely.

I've been wanting to summarize all these experiences, to lay down a blueprint for creating unconditional money and love in your life. Today I see that I would only be building you another cage. The truth is much bigger than cages.

The truth is that there are a million ways to create love and money, a million ways to fly your dreams and live without limitation. I have stumbled over a few of them. I have had the privilege of meeting people who are living differently, who have made their own assumptions about money and life. I have had the opportunity to play with their ideas, to push through some of my fears, to experiment with new relationships to life.

For that, I am profoundly grateful.

Today, as this drunken symphony pours through me, and a million blueprints wind their way across reality, there's only one assumption I would like to share with you. Life is bigger than you can imagine; the possibilities are endless. There's no need to limit yourself to whatever patterns you've inherited or learned. Get out in life and PLAY!

I have played with my assumptions about spirit and matter, followed each one down into the other, like the spiraling ends of yin and yang, and found that both of them are only different facets of a single whole. One is not more holy than the other. One is not more troublesome or dense.

Money flows from any source you let it. So does love, and joy, and freedom. Every part of you has infinite creative power. Let life do its work!

I've smudged the boundary between my inner male and female, found that both those attitudes and energies have an essential role to play in my relationship with life. I must surrender openly to life at times; at times I must be active and focused and firm. It's up to me to decide which tool to use when. If I only use one, I'll spend my life running in circles, one foot nailed to the floor, in a prison that doesn't need walls.

Another cage was the relationship between my inner child and inner parent. Part of me feels helpless and abandoned; part of me feels overburdened and responsible. These two parts have victimized each other ever since I can remember, tossing back and forth the blame for every failure.

Once I stopped judging myself as a failure, they had nothing to fight about. Now they're learning to get along, on a deep emotional level. Sometimes I need comforting and reassurance, and sometimes I need to feel strong and capable. They each take their turn now, and no one feels left out. I stopped making either of them the core of my identity; they're only facets of a bigger whole.

Reuniting opposites: that has been a key for me, perhaps the central key in all of this. I used to spend my life deciding between opposites: will I be spiritual or worldly? open or closed? vulnerable or safe? rich or poor?

Now I embrace both sides equally. I line up with heaven and earth. What a waste of time it was deciding which was more important! As if either could exist without the other...

My journey led me out of slavery and into choice. Work and play are differences of attitude. If I feel I have no choice about what I'm doing -- even if it's the most delightful thing I can imagine -- eventually it turns to drudgery and work. If I always give myself permission to get up and leave, no situation ever feels intolerable. There are always other ways to make life happen.

There's no one way to make money in the world; there are no rules that bind you to a single pathway or career. The old world was externally-based, and it could afford to be, because external circumstances changed so very slowly, over generations. The new world we're creating changes from decade to decade, and in some fields, even faster. If you can't adapt, you're obsolete.

Our money and financial systems will be changing, too. Some will fall apart; some, take new forms. Embracing cocreation brings us into a flow that's much deeper than dollars and yen. Unconditional abundance is bigger than banks. No matter where we go, or what the circumstances, we can ride the waves, and play with what's at hand. Money magicians can turn anything to gold!

Taking your lead from the outer world will always put you at a disadvantage, because in that dance, you'll always be one step behind. The people I have met who move the most money are the people who play the tune. It doesn't take a lot of clout or power to play your own tune. It just takes a lot of courage and nerve.

This cage-rattling hurricane I'm in today feels like another step in that direction.

The wind is howling, the ground is shaking, a thousand voices scream and wail in a thousand different keys. The safety of my cage is being torn apart; a pit is opening beneath my feet.

There is no single truth, about anything. There is no single road to wealth, despite what anyone may say. I've seen too many people take too many different paths, and reach their goals. Success is not dependent on following instructions; we're not in school any more.

We're in a free-form universe, and every person makes their own reality. Day by day, minute by minute, we create our own paths through the wilderness. We can use whatever tools we choose. We can lead or follow, or do both in turn. We can inherit our lessons, make them up, or co-create a new reality. The choice is ours.

Unconditional money, like unconditional love, means living free from expectations and conditions. It is a vast and profound allowing, in which life becomes a partner in the process, not an adversary or a distant god.

When I live unconditionally, life transforms into a grand adventure. I find a balance between all the oppositions, and I dance between them, on that razor's edge. Money flows because I love myself, and I support the dance I am creating. Life mirrors my attitude -- no, more than that: life falls in love with what I am creating.

I used to witness life, admire and react to its creations, try to add my energies to the ongoing song. Now I'm on the stage myself, making it up as I go, and life is in the front row, watching me, jaw hanging open with wonder and surprise. If I ask for a back-up, life jumps to the piano to play harmony; if I ask for a hat, life hands me its own hat, or conjures one up out of nothing. Life doesn't want to interrupt the show. It will do anything I ask; it wants to see where I am going with this song-and-dance.

Life loves nothing more than someone who is living, and living to the limit. When I'm alive, and in the flow of love and joy and creativity, then everyone supports me, no one resists. It's the most awesome power in the universe, and it is mine to use for whatever I want. Money's just a pale reflection of that power, that support, that love. As I get out of my own way, and drop the old assumptions that life doesn't care, then I allow life to participate with me in making something new. That's life. That's love.

That's power.

And that, my friends, is Unconditional Money.

The music is in you; the money's in your hands. The instant you decide to play with life instead of struggling and fighting it, the magic begins.

Thank you for your patience and support. Thank you for playing the audience to my improvised show. I hope that when you leave this book, you'll be humming a few of these songs. I hope you feel inspired to sing them in the shower, in the privacy of your home, and -- eventually, as you become accustomed to the magical power of your own unique voice -- from the very rooftops of the world.

Blessings on you, each and every one. As you bring your dreams into reality, I give you the greatest blessing I know: May your life become a grand and unconditional adventure!

Photo by Glen Hashitani

TO CONTACT THE AUTHOR:
Please write David Cates, PO Box 1100, Willamina, OR 97396.
Or you can e-mail to: DCates1111@aol.com.

TO CONTACT BUFFALO PRESS:
To order additional copies of *Unconditional Money*,
or be informed of upcoming workshops, events and titles
(like the *Unconditional Money Guidebook for Money Magicians*),
please send your request to:
Buffalo Press, PO Box 40, Willamina, OR 97396,
or fax us at (503) 876-3800.

AFTERWORD

I made another trip to California after that, to tap into the world of publishing. I spent two months there, playing, attending conferences, meeting people. I didn't care for what I found.

Everyone I met did business the old way. They were working for a living, caught up in status and roles, keeping score. They moved solid product in a solid world.

I didn't want to play with them.

Meanwhile, JF found me a new laptop, just by asking around. Someone gave it to him. He passed it on to me. Suddenly, I was completely mobile.

I liked that.

I gave up my classes and my house. I did my consultations on the phone, from wherever I happened to be. I carried this book, and others, around in my laptop. I could write on a mountaintop, by the Golden Gate Bridge, at a ski chalet, in a friend's garden.

The unseen hurricane blew me to California, up to Washington, over to Utah. When people asked me where I lived, I told them, "The West Coast."

Along the way, I made a lot of friends. I have the keys to twenty-seven homes. I am a part of many families, who ask nothing from me but my presence. Forget about earning and work; now I don't even have to play! I can sit in the corner and write, if I want, and that's enough.

Life continues to provide, no matter how outrageously I stretch it...

In time, I circled in on Oregon again. One evening I stayed with JF and Joyce, at their place in the country. That night it snowed. I had a dream that JF published *Unconditional Money*.

In the morning, I asked him if he wanted to do that in real

life. Neither of us had ever published anything before. Neither of us knew what we were doing.

He said, "Yes."

Actually, it was a bit more tearful and emotional than that, but the end result was "Yes."

And so, JF created Buffalo Press, and I commenced to finish this book up on the laptop he had given me.

Shortly after that, at a weekend band practice, doing what he loved, JF met a millionaire who lived out in the woods and played guitar. This guy had made his fortune in publishing, and volunteered to show JF the ropes. He shared distribution tips, accounting programs, reference guides.

Other people, ordinary people, wanted to participate in the unfolding magic. We offered shares in this new business venture to raise capital for printing.

After all the painful lessons we'd created for each other, JF and I had come around, full circle. Here he was again, supporting this book, in a way that neither one of us could ever have envisioned in Hawaii when we started this adventure. In Hawaii, where I was a butler, and he washed cars.

Which only goes to show you, if you're really willing to play, anything can happen...

YOUR INVITATION

Once upon a time, a reader very much like you decided to co-create a life of unconditional abundance. Inspired by this book, she found her own pathway, fought her own inner fears, and learned extraordinary lessons about life. As a gift of gratitude, and a testimony to her own success, she wrote about her greatest moment in a letter that she mailed to me.

When her anecdote arrived here in the coastal woods of Oregon, I celebrated with her, delighted for her growth and courage. I took her story on the road with me, as a permanent part of my heart. If you come to hear me speak some day, you might hear me repeat it.

JF and I tucked her letter away in a very special carved wooden box, along with all the other true-life tales of inspiration sent by other readers. When the time is ripe, we hope to publish some of these turning points in a sequel to *Unconditional Money*.

All across the country, the magic is spreading. In private lives, in businesses, in organizations of every size and purpose, we are learning to make money with passion and integrity.

We invite you to send your inspiring anecdotes to us, so that we can share them with others. We want to hear how you're playing with the magic.

Send your brief selection to:

True Stories
Buffalo Press
PO Box 1100
Willamina, OR 97396

Thanks for playing with us!